"Eddie has identified the keys to creating a successful online business and explains how you can build any idea into on~~line~~

Penny Power OBI

12

Startup Success Secrets

Mindset and Strategies workbook for building a Successful Online Business

EDDIE YU

12 Startup Success Secrets

First published in 2014 by

Panoma Press
48 St Vincent Drive, St Albans, Herts, AL1 5SJ, UK
info@panomapress.com
www.panomapress.com

Book layout by Neil Coe

Printed on acid-free paper from managed forests.

ISBN 978-1-909623-74-3

Dedication

For my family who have never understood what I do for a living but have always been there in times of need.

Contents

Preface

Thank you for picking up this book and reading this introduction. Wherever you might be right now, in a bookshop or sitting at home online, the fact that you started to look at this book means that at some unconscious level, there's something you want to learn from it.

All our actions are intentional, whether we consciously choose to act in a certain way, or some unconscious action occurs automatically, all our actions have a reason behind them. The really important thing to understand is that you have a conscious choice to act when it comes to creating direction in your life, so the action you've taken to pick this book up is just the beginning of your journey of learning.

Congratulations also for choosing the path of learning. In life, learning is one of the most important values that we should all embrace because it's the path to greater wisdom, which in my mind is the application of knowledge to create positive outcomes.

As a species we are fantastic learning machines, from the beginning when we were just groupings of cells, we learnt how to improve our cell groupings to ensure survival. As cell groupings became more complex, we began to evolve and grow bodies and arms and legs, eventually evolving into the human beings that we are today, all through learning and adaptation. As cavemen we learnt how to make fire and hunt for food and as mankind continued to evolve, we learnt about the world around us and what makes us human and what makes the universe what it is today.

We cannot stop learning, however in modern day society I've discovered that many people either limit themselves by saying they aren't great learners, or people refuse to learn because they cannot see the value of it.

I think that is a real shame, but for you, reading this book is going to give you some incredible insights into how you can successfully get into the head space of setting up and running an internet based business.

Let me start the book by clarifying that I'm not a business guru, nor am I a multi-millionaire. Equally I don't claim to be an expert internet entrepreneur as there are many people who know so much more than me in terms of internet businesses. In the 13 years I've been working at this, there have been many geniuses in the world that have created global billion dollar businesses online such as Facebook, YouTube, Twitter and many others.

I am, however, free from the confines of corporate employment, and I'm financially and spiritually free to live life the way I choose to. What I am hoping to share with you is how you can also create this kind of lifestyle for yourself, knowing that if I can do it, so can you.

I must also advise that this is not a technical book, so if you are expecting some sort of technical manual to internet business then you're better off buying one of the many technical magazines on newsagents' shelves.

This is a book about mindset and strategy. Mindset is the level of conscious and unconscious thinking which controls your actions that produces the results you get in life. Whether those results are good or bad for you is merely a consequence of your thoughts, so changing your mindset will alter your results dramatically.

This book is also a doing book. What I mean by this is that there are powerful workshop exercises to do, to help you to get more out of the knowledge contained within. Personally I find that I learn best by doing, so if you also learn best this way, you'll enjoy the workshop exercises. If you prefer to read the whole book first, come back later to work on your internet business using the exercises.

The strategy is the methodology of how to marry the mindset with clear actions so that you can replicate the results other people have achieved. You might have a great mindset to begin with but if you don't have a clear strategy then you might latch onto strategies that don't work for you, which often lead to disheartened attempts at entrepreneurship.

I've seen people take on strategies within the trading of stocks, shares, commodities or options, and for the most part they've had to pay for the knowledge. The teachers of these programs are delivering great knowledge, however the fundamental mistake people make is they think they can make themselves passionate about this because it "makes money". These strategies only work if you already have an interest in financial markets.

What you need to do is to learn the overarching strategies (meta-strategy) of someone successful and apply it to what you are passionate about. Only then will you get the results you're looking for, doing what you love the most, and living a life worth living.

What I love most about being in business online is that it levels the playing field, allowing small operations to compete with the established companies in the market. It is also a fundamental paradigm shift back to how trade was originally conceptualized when tribesmen were working to serve their tribe.

In the early days of human society, people conducted their business in their own space, whether that is inside their own homes or in an additional workspace created at home. As humans progressed, and civilization advanced, people began grouping together to achieve more. They congregated in markets to sell products and services to each other. They gathered to collaborate on big ideas and formed central places of work to facilitate greater efficiency and better results. The driver behind all these shifts was the need to communicate instantly, which in past times would have meant meeting in person.

Even in the modern era as the industrial age took place and various technological advancements including the telephone and computers came about, people still gathered in large offices to facilitate the efficient course of business.

Since 2006, there have been countless technological advances which means that we can now effectively communicate with anyone on the planet at any time. Taking us right back, giving us the ability to work like tribesmen, in our own spaces, yet have the capability of instant global communication, the kind which brought humans together in the first place.

Now that we have this powerful mechanism to communicate through the internet via our mobile devices and computers, I firmly believe that society is moving back towards a place where offices will no longer be necessary for business, a model of dispersed working that hasn't been seen before. Think about the ramifications for society, less commuting, less office space (which is left empty at night, draining the world's resources), greater happiness for everyone because every individual will have greater degrees of autonomy.

I've taken the first steps in making this a reality for me, so I hope that you can learn about the successes and failures I've had in 13 years and maybe you too can apply the strategies within this book to something you love doing so that you can create an internet-based business that works for your lifestyle.

I'd like to thank the following people who have been a part of my life and made this reality possible with their support, knowledge and guidance.

- My family, Fred Weiss, Peter Rolls, Andy Tiong, Tarek Naja, Scott Jaeger, Emma Harvey, Andrew Hunt, Candice Eley, Mindy Gibbins-Klein, Daniel Priestley, Lazo Freeman, Christopher Howard, Duane Alley, Amy Brann, Esther Zheng, Kam Uppal, Owen Lean, David Wygant

I'd also like to thank the following people for continuing to inspire me with their incredible life stories and work.

- Sir Richard Branson, Anthony Robbins, Dalai Lama, Eben Pagan, Sean Stephenson, Oprah Winfrey, Lord Alan Sugar, Mark Zuckerberg, Bill Gates, Bob Proctor, Will Smith, Simon Cowell, Jeremy Gilley

Introduction: Speedlights, visas and a billion-dollar industry

The day had arrived, after months of preparation I was sitting in my lounge looking down on a table where I could see all my equipment ready for the day ahead. Amongst the items I had on the table there were radio triggers, soft boxes, spare batteries and various lenses that I needed to use for the shoot.

But amongst them all, my favourite item was the speedlight because it can be used really creatively to create images that are striking and a lot of fun. It's a fast and furious piece of equipment that gives photos a sharper, glitzier edge. The speedlight gave me unlimited creative potential when it came to photography because I was not longer confined to just using natural light. I could create my own environment, light the subjects my own way and create an even more inspired image as a result.

Anyway, today had been a culmination of several months' planning, finding the right people to work with and doing phone interviews with models that might suit the role that we were casting for. This was all new to me because today was the first time that I would be doing a full production fashion shoot.

I had agreed to help a friend and colleague out with their new advertising images for their hair salon. What they needed was a set of iconic photos that would demonstrate their excellence in hair design. To achieve this, I had organised a full production shoot over several months and gathered four models, a makeup artist, two wardrobe stylists and a their team of nine hair stylists.

To say I was excited might be an understatement for I was ecstatic about the day ahead. Don't get me wrong, I was also terrified at the same time, but overall the adrenaline kicked in from the moment I woke up and fired me up for the day. I wanted to get great results that day so I got my equipment packed and ready in the car and set off to the hair salon where the preparations would begin.

It was only a short car ride away, about 10 minutes, but in these 10 minutes I became even more excited as I got nearer and started to see activity in the salon already. Parking up, I eagerly got out and grabbed a few bags knowing that this was going to be one hell of a day...

...I walked closer and geared myself up, it was a day that I knew wouldn't be repeated again, I opened the door and I saw the dim lights of the computer screen shining up at a frustrated face. I had come to help solve a mission critical problem.

The software for this large bank's trading system had faulted and at a level that meant that it was both mission critical and losing money whilst the system was down.

I immediately started work with the guy to solve the problem and got myself settled in for I knew that this would be a long day. The company who produced the software, for whom I worked at the time, had their headquarters in Philadelphia, so being in the UK, I was on my own for a while until the USA woke up from their slumber to hear of the problem.

What was frustrating was that there were almost no clues as to what went wrong; throughout the trouble testing, I was going back and forth with the core developers in Philadelphia, who were literally trying to figure out the problem remotely with me on the London end where the problem was.

These were the days when the internet was still fairly slow, so forget transferring large files over broadband; it was a case of little by little which of course made the whole situation even more frustrating. At the same time, I was also facing the bank's senior executives bashing my ear about the situation getting worse.

It was just one of those days and I knew that this wasn't what I wanted in my life. I was frustrated, but for what? I was a cog in a big complex system, which wasn't part of my dream. I got so frustrated that, late afternoon, I stepped outside for fresh air and, out of frustration and pure spontaneity, I picked up my phone and booked a trip to Egypt. I had been eyeing this trip for a couple of weeks. I wanted to do something different, outside my comfort zone, and a backpacking trip for 3 weeks across Egypt was most definitely outside my comfort zone at the time.

I couldn't believe what I had done, but I had to get back to the server room because there was still the immediate problem at hand. Following a few more back and forth fixes with head office, we discovered the root causes of the issues.

The problem at the bank was resolved by the end of the day, it was my longest working day I ever had – 17 hours of painstaking frustration, eventually solved. I ended up leaving for Egypt 2 weeks after that incident at the bank and I whilst on the plane I remembered the circumstances that led me to being there. As I landed in Cairo airport, late at night because we were the last flight in, I gathered my backpack ready for an adventure, but there was one last hurdle.

Being a novice traveller, I had forgotten to get a visa! However, at Cairo airport you can 'buy' a visa from the foreign currency exchange desk. It was all very dodgy and I started to feel some trepidation. Here I was on an adventure, outside my comfort zone and now I didn't have a proper entry visa. So I plucked up the courage and got what I think was actually just a black market visa and headed towards immigration.

They looked at the visa, the British passport and then, looking at me without question, they took me to a room and said they needed to check my passport; I knew they had seen me getting the visa from the dodgy exchange desk. I sat down, in this empty room in Cairo airport, almost midnight, with no passport now, and I wondered what on earth I had gotten myself into...

...As I looked up towards the ceiling, I could see the dim illumination of the computer lighting it up. It was another late night of surfing the internet looking for answers to my predicament.

I had quit that job with the Philadelphia software company almost 9 months ago, and I had gone to Egypt and back. I had quit that job and made a decision to redesign my life, so I took time off and technically I was unemployed, but things weren't great. Although I had some savings, I was rapidly entering five figures worth of debt and I needed a plan. I was curious to find out what opportunities there might be online.

As I surfed around the internet on my slow connection, I came across an interesting article on Yahoo news and my curiosity was stepped up a gear. I first noticed the graph, which showed affiliate marketing growing to the billion dollar mark and I started to read the rest of the article content.

It was an incredibly interesting article about the rise of this new industry, focused around the industry of online gambling. At that time, both online gambling and affiliate marketing were really new concepts, and there wasn't much information online about them. Still this article showed incredible promise and armed with my intense curiosity about it all, I went on a journey of discovery online. One article led to another, which led to other websites that gave me a lot of research about this new marketing method. Somewhere along the way through my research and reading, I had decided to pursue it as a serious business.

My curiosity continued as I investigated the main competitors in the market. I wanted to see if there was an opening for me to explore. It wasn't long after doing my due diligence that I knew I could do better than the competition and now I wanted to know whether I could pull it off. The only way to know was to try, so without further thought I began the journey of a lifetime.

Several months later, sat at the same desk, I was looking at my very first commercial website and wondering what life had in store for me as I day dreamed about a time in the future when I would be free from working for other people, free from working for "The Boss".

SECRET 1

Live a Life Worth Living

What we all strive to achieve in life is some sort of fulfilment and purpose and ultimately happiness that we are living a good life and one that makes sense to us. Being an internet entrepreneur, I know how it feels to be on both sides of the fence because I didn't just fall into being an entrepreneur, I worked my backside off in jobs which I thought I wanted to do, but when I started to become much more self aware, I realised that they were not.

In fact you might be in the same place also right now because you are considering setting up some sort of new venture and you're looking into the online avenue as a possible path. Let me tell you, this was the best thing I ever did. It wasn't easy to make that transition from employee to entrepreneur and then make a success out of it; the lifestyle that I now lead is something that most people would dream of, but it's something I worked hard over the last 13 years to create.

In 2008 I embarked on an epic adventure of self-discovery that ultimately led to a world trip that I began in November 2009. In this trip, which was to take place over 1 month, I would visit seven cities around the world, do five different fashion photo shoots and meet with friends in every city I passed through. It was an absolute whirlwind tour, which took me from the dizzying streets of New York, to the calm tranquil beaches in Fiji. There was one reason why I was undertaking such a trip, and it was due to the fact that I had signed up for a mindset training retreat, which was to take place in the Sheraton Hotel on Denarau Island in Fiji.

This training was one that would teach us how to dissect the way billionaires think, down to their behaviour patterns, their strategies, their attitudes and values in life. These core principles are what makes these people highly successful, delivering natural value with everything they do.

This was certainly something that I wanted to learn about and even though the cost of the trip was massive, it was something that I knew would be a long-term investment into my own mind, which is the controlling mechanism that determines whether or not I succeed in my own life.

So the trip was a great big adventure, both challenging, as I had some amazing times within the world of fashion photography, and revealing, as I learnt a lot more about myself and what makes me tick.

Suffice to say, this was a trip that I hadn't imagined I'd ever be doing, nor even have the finances to do when I first started out in developing my own internet business. However, what I'm saying is that when you have the right attitudes and determination in life, you can make anything succeed and it all starts in the mind.

Money buys you choices

It's not about the money, it's all about the choices we have in life and you are at a choice point right now. We all want to earn and make more money, but that's because we all have dreams and ideals, and in order to fulfil those dreams and ideals we need money.

We live in a world with an economy which runs on the trading of value and that's why money is important; it's the mechanism which allows us to trade our own skill and value for something that represents that value that we can then trade with someone else. Hopefully that someone else is helping you towards your dreams, and not just helping you flipping out and buying really extravagant things for the sake of it.

I'm sure you've heard the stories of lottery millionaires who lose all their money within a few years of winning, simply because they don't respect the money, as they haven't earned it themselves.

What I'm saying here is that it's important to value and respect money, not because you've got dollar signs in your eyes, but because it's the mechanism which will allow you to increase the choices you have in life and buy the experiences which will bring you joy and happiness.

The choices it buys you are those that will stay with you for the rest of your life. You know this to be true because up till now, you've probably not had much choice and you've followed the path that's been laid down before you.

What I'm telling you is that there are now multiple choices for you to make. You may choose to stop reading this book, for example, and get really excited about going out there to find what you can do online, or you could immediately get out a piece of paper and start to brainstorm what you could do as an online business. However, I urge you to read through this whole book so that you can learn from my experience, my mistakes and shortcut all those things that I painstakingly went through because I didn't have a guide when I first started.

Focus on what you really want

It's important to dream.

When we were children we used to dream all the time and for many those dreams were squashed by parents, society or peers.

Do you know why it's so important to dream? Because the most incredible things happen when you dream and you believe in your own dream.

If the Wright Bros didn't dream of flying, we wouldn't have airplanes today. If Henry Ford didn't dream that it would be possible to mass produce cars in the thousands, we wouldn't have vehicles that help us in so many ways today.

Imagine if Thomas Edison didn't dream that he could harness the power of light into a bulb. We might still be burning flames to bring light, and I certainly wouldn't have as much fun without my speedlight for photography.

You see, some of the most profound inventions in history have all been made on the back of dreams and strong belief that it would be possible.

When you dream, you start to place things into your mind that otherwise wouldn't have been there, and because you've placed them there, your mind can't actually tell the difference between an imagined thought and the real thing.

I find that so interesting, that the mind can't actually tell what is real or what is imagined. It's all just a bunch of neurons firing electrical patterns that make up our memories.

When you know something to be true, you behave differently towards it. For example, if you knew that the deal you were working on would be guaranteed success upon its conclusion, you'd work towards it with utter conviction and confidence that nothing could go wrong; everything you did would be the right and perfect thing to do, because you knew for certain the outcome.

If you didn't believe that the outcome would be good, then your behaviours and attitudes would be different. You would probably be a little complacent, maybe lazy, perhaps even making rash decisions without thinking twice about it.

Now we all know which way of approaching this deal would work the best, the former of course. So holding that firm belief that you will succeed and that firm thought of what you really want will ultimately dictate a lot of your unconscious actions towards the right direction, without you even needing to think about it.

This is a powerful concept to understand because when you can align your conscious and unconscious minds and have them working as one, you can achieve incredible results.

For myself, one of the things that I kept my eye on right at the beginning was the freedom to live my life the way I choose to. I remember quite early, before I was actually making any money online, that I set myself a goal of making £10,000 a month, but it wasn't just that I set the goal and let it be, I totally and utterly believed that it would be possible and I never let anything get in the way of my belief.

Yes, plenty of people told me it would be impossible, from my friends to my parents, all people whom I trusted and loved, yet none of them supported my belief, I felt like Dumbo at times. However, I never stopped believing it was possible because I had already met people who were earning this amount from online businesses of their own, and I knew that if they could do it, I could as well. It was only a matter of finding out how it was done and then implementing the strategy.

It wasn't just enough to set the goal, I had also verbally told people that this was what I was setting out to achieve. This gave me added accountability because I didn't want to suffer the ridicule that they would give me if I failed.

I tell you that story just to illustrate how vital it is to stay true to your beliefs. What I would advise these days is to keep in mind more visual goals like the dream holiday you've wanted, or a home of your own, and keep these in mind as your goals. These are much more powerful than some financial figure. I know this now having learnt a lot from my own past experiences and I hope that you'll learn this too.

I've already mentioned how fortunate I have been in taking that world trip. Did I mention that I did that whole trip in 28 days in business class as well? I'm not saying this to gloat, I'm telling you because it's true and all of this was achieved simply by building a successful online business, and if I can do it, so can you.

I'm not a genius, nor some programming expert, nor a marketing guru, in fact I had zero marketing knowhow and had to learn all of that from scratch. I'm saying that whatever you want to do, it can be learnt.

I use vision boards and now a vision journal to hold images of all my dreams and goals; this keeps me on track to keep achieving the things I want in my life. Question is, what do you really want for yourself?

Opportunity to build long term wealth

We all know that the way to long term success is to build sustainable wealth in investments that grow over time. The fact of the matter is, it takes a fair amount of capital to get investments underway and being able to build this capital from online business can in the long run enable you to invest wisely and create wealth vehicles that will drive you forward into the future.

My mother always said to me that it takes money to make money and that is so true when it comes to serious sustainable wealth. Having a successful online business will allow you to diversify your funds into these investment vehicles that means you don't have to worry about your financial situation.

When I talk about wealth, I'm not just talking about financial wealth. I'm also talking about spiritual wealth and wealth of knowledge. Another important investment to make when you start to have money is the investment you put back into yourself. You'll be able to go away and learn all those things that you wanted to, because not only will you have the money to do it, you'll also have the freedom and time to do it.

It's amazing to think that these days I've had opportunities to learn so many different things because of building a successful online business. I've learnt professional photography to a level where I can now direct full production fashion shoots. My curiosity in human achievement led me to learn neuro-linguistic programming and I've since become trained in hypnosis and NLP, which allows me to deliver life and business coaching with even better results.

My mind has been nourished by the knowledge with which I eagerly consume. All because of a great internet business. I'm telling you this because I know that you can do it too, and that when it comes to building an online business, I can give you all the advice currently in my mind, so that you can avoid all the things that held me back.

When it comes to the ultimate investment for long-term wealth, I've also been able to use the money I've earned to invest into properties, which has allowed me to build a nice property portfolio that is itself an income-generating system. The opportunities came about when I met my first property mentor and he taught me a strategy called buy-to-let. This allowed me to leverage my existing property and purchase other properties with a view to letting them out. Taking this on board, I've managed to build my own portfolio, which today almost runs itself now.

By now you might be wondering why I'm telling you a bunch of stories and not getting into the technical aspects of online businesses. Well there's a very good reason; you must train your mindset first, before you implement your plan. In fact I'd say as much as 80% of the success I had was due to having the right mindset, but for me, that mindset was something I toiled night and day to sculpt because I didn't know any better. I didn't read books to help me, I didn't take courses, and I certainly didn't enrol the help of others. I literally did things the hardest way possible, and really, there's no need now in today's market where there are plenty of ways to shortcut the most painful parts of my own journey.

Life is for living, go crazy, have fun and splash out

I've already talked about having and maintaining those dreams, and I'm sure that some of those are material things like expensive toys, fast cars or lavish jewellery. I absolutely encourage you to have these dreams, as well as all the nice stuff like contributing to charity, and helping out the family.

We are, after all, human and what we all seek is happiness, in all its many forms. I know that many of those forms come in rewards; treating yourself and having fun whilst you build this new online business is absolutely vital to your own happiness.

It serves as an incentive for you to carry on, a reminder that what you are doing is good for you, good for people around you and achieves what you want.

It's all about balance – as well as all the good advice about investing in the long term and building solid grounds for why you are pursuing this course, I'm also saying you need to go and have fun. When you start to make money online, by Zeus' beard, go reward yourself!

I have lots of fun, perhaps too much in the early days of success, for there was a period of time when I would go out and spend too much money on champagne nights with my friends. They loved me for it! I guess it was all just fun and laughs, and even though I look back and think how much it all cost me, I know now that it was all part of the learning and part of the fun of becoming a successful online entrepreneur.

I drive a Porsche 911 these days, my dream car since a young age and I've been on vacations all around the world. This is all made possible because of the internet, I'm not saying this because I'm showing off, well maybe a little, but I am really telling you because I sincerely believe that you can do it too. I believe in it so much that I've built my business around this now, and my core business is helping people to start online business ventures and making them successful. This book tells you how I did it, how you can do it and what the key concepts are to make it happen for you.

Freedom to work how and when you choose

I hated being stuck in a 9-5 job. It was something that I wanted to get out of, and creating an online business allowed me to do that. It gave me the freedom to work anytime I wanted; to live life the way I choose to. It allows you to make time to do the things you enjoy the most at times that suit you.

I've been able to learn salsa dancing and photography as I've mentioned already, all because my time it flexible and under my own control.

It's a powerful position to be in, because it allows you to find the pattern that works best for you. Some people do work better in the mornings and some people are better workers at night. Some people work best in 2-hour slots with 1-hour breaks in between, some people work best in 4-hour blocks.

Working an online business means you can find the pattern that you work best to, and then in the other times you allocate, you can do things to relax or to energise yourself. A pattern that should be mentioned here is the Ultradian Rhythm that can be adapted for peak work performance.

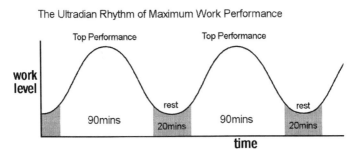

The Ultradian Rhythm is a natural human cycle that occurs throughout the day. The human mind can focus and concentrate for 90 to 120 minutes at a time and work with sustained energy after which our attention span decreases and we need to take a break for at least 15 -20 minutes before we can focus once again.

During this 20 minute period of 'low energy' you are likely to feel sleepy and may find it difficult to concentrate and focus on your work. Most people try to divert their mind by having a cup of tea, coffee or cigarette. Though this may make you feel better for a short while, it increases the stress levels and has an adverse effect on your health.

To use this to your advantage you need to understand the Ultradian Rhythm and use the downtime in a way that it energizes you without indulging in harmful actions. The important thing about this break is that you don't talk or think about the task you were engaged in, just go and do something completely different. In fact, any change will do the trick, so long as we really take a complete break. This will have you returning to your work, revitalized and calm, ready to take on the next piece of work with a refreshed mind.

Remember that you will perform any task more effectively if you take a 20-minute break every 90-minutes or so. But, many times this may not be possible when people are engaged in important sessions and meetings and taking a break becomes difficult.

You are in complete control of your own time, which means you are ultimately responsible for yourself. This does mean that once you've found the way of working which produces maximum results for you, that you must stick to it and plan your time accordingly.

The responsibility for your own success lies only with you. Your employer no longer has any part to play in the planning of your time, so any poor planning on your part would lead to failure.

One method I use all the time is to plan to do the most valuable things first. What I mean by this is find out those tasks that make the maximum impact to your new business venture, and spend most of your time doing those tasks first.

You'll hear me talking a lot about the 80/20 rule or also known as the Pareto Principle. It's true to say that 80% of your success is going to come down to 20% of the things you do.

That's not to say that the other 80% of tasks aren't important, they are. It's the combined effort that makes the difference, what I mean in this case is that 20% of the tasks you do, are the actual ones that will change the course of your business for the better, so concentrate on doing those first!

Success online leads to life fulfilment

Ok, I'm not going to ramble on about being fulfilled in life because that gets into a whole different philosophical debate about what makes people happy. I am going to say that it really makes you a lot happier and when you are happy, your joy will overflow to those around you and the knock on effect of that is powerful indeed.

Teach someone everything

I've met people along the way who've wanted to learn and one thing I learnt from a mentor is that when you become successful, teach others what you know, and he even suggested taking on board someone as an apprentice and teaching them everything you know for free.

I must admit that I was sceptical about this, however I've come to understand the importance of sharing knowledge and I've also taught several people everything I know. This has led me to fine tune my craft even more, so that when I'm teaching, I'm sure that what I teach is correct and going to work. It's like using a sharpening blade for knives, the knife is already sharp and I'm just making sure the fine edge is kept totally sharp.

Another way to think about it is if you do come across someone who is keen and eager to learn, and you don't do what you can to teach them the right way to do it, they may well go away and learn the incorrect way of doing it. I do believe in karma, so this could come back to bite you on the backside.

Learning about your highest values

After you've been concentrating on your business for an extended period of time, or perhaps once all the partying is over (success brings parties for sure!), you'll also have time to reflect on your own success and possibly where you've failed. These are the most important lessons of all. You get to learn about yourself and what drives you. You'll learn your highest and most core value that you hold true in your heart. I know for me this has been an incredible journey so far. I've gone from a shy, introverted technician to a publicly profiled entrepreneur and I've discovered that there is so much more to me that I had been led to believe.

This has led to improved family relationships, better communication between friends and finding love in a loveless society.

If you want to discover a little more about yourself, do this test that I did a while back to find out what it is that I really want. It was taught to me by a respected mentor of mine, and then I added a small twist to make it even more powerful.

Write down on a piece of paper 100 goals. These can be things you want to buy: toys, experiences, vacations, houses, anything at all. From wanting to visit the Pyramids, through to wanting a family or perhaps grandchildren. Don't stop until you reach 100.

When you do, go through each item on the list and ask yourself why you want that item you wrote down. Spend some time on this because this is the important part. Once you've written down a few sentences why you wanted that item, for all 100 items, you will discover something about yourself that is so true and core, that it will shake your very mindset into the right mode.

When I did this, I discovered that even within a lot of the materialistic things on my list, and the great experiences in life, my fundamental value that I hold dear was creativity.

When I discovered this and looked back at all the things I had done in my life leading up to that point, I realised and noticed that all the things I was best at since childhood, were all creative things. By the way, you can be creative artistically as well as technically.

I hope you'll do this exercise because I know that it will make a profound difference in your life.

The importance of contribution

I briefly mentioned about helping to mentor someone and teach him what you know. This helps you to hone your own craft as well as share with others. What is also important is contributing back to society, whether that is with your own time or money, or the skills you now have.

Economies, societies, people and business are all one deeply interlinked organic system, and so is the internet. Something amazing happens when you give back to society, it's called the law of reciprocity and I do know for a fact that when you give unselfishly, you will receive in abundance.

I came across this notion when I first read Tony Robbins and one of the things he always talks about in his seven keys to success is contribution. At that time I hadn't even thought about this and for sure it was missing in my own life strategy. Seeing as I had done most of the other six mentioned, I figured he must be onto something, so I gave contribution a go.

What I did to contribute initially was to give my time to organizing events for people via a social networking website. It had nothing to do with my business and all I wanted to do was to just help others. It was quite easy; all I did was arrange social events like outings, restaurant evenings and social gatherings.

I didn't expect anything in return and certainly there was no motive at all other than giving my time away. What I got in return was to me unbelievable. I just hadn't come across this law of reciprocity, so when it started to payback, I started to understand the organic nature of life and how everything is literally connected. Do good and good will come back to you.

So from doing this bit of organizing for other people, I've gotten new joint venture agreements, made new friends for life, received valuable business advice, met incredibly talented people whom I wouldn't have had a chance to meet otherwise, and received more clients.

I went on further and affiliated myself with Action Aid sponsoring children in the poorest areas of the planet. I'm also privileged to be a patron of the Peace One Day movement, and it just seems the more I give, the more opportunities come my way. I've had inspired talks with top multi-million pound entrepreneurs, made powerful joint ventures and met some of the most inspirational people on the planet and even been in the presence of the Dalai Lama.

Giving is like an elastic band that stretches your boundaries. You can give a little and you'll get back a little, or you can give a lot and you'll also get a lot back, but your boundaries will also be stretched a little more each time, allowing you to encompass more around you and growing yourself as an individual, as well as your business interests, exponentially.

How amazing can your life become?

So I've told you a bunch of stories, and some of them are a little wild and perhaps even egotistical. You might think that I'm just showing off, but that's not the point, I told these stories because I wanted to make the point about how amazing your life could be too when you put your mind at work and take your own internet business seriously.

I want you to imagine what life would be like when you've made your own business success online, and think about what would happen if you didn't do it.

Keep asking yourself the question, how amazing can my life be when I put my mind to it, and I hope you'll agree with me that when you really put your mind to it, your life can be even more amazing than mine.

Workshop 1: Setting your goals

Spend a few moments to write down your answers to the following questions:

1) Why are you thinking of starting an internet business? What are all the reasons pointing you towards this direction?

2) Ask yourself what would happen if you didn't setup your own internet business?

3) Now ask yourself what would happen if you did.

4) What is your intention for reading this book, what do you hope to learn? Take those intentions and set them as your goal, your outcome for reading this book and that will give you clarity of thought as you read.

5) Now ask yourself what goal you can set yourself for 1 year's time that would mean you had made positive changes towards the lifestyle of your choice.

6) Now set yourself a goal of what you want to have achieved in 1 month's time in relation to your internet business.

Notes

SECRET 2

The Internet Changes the Entrepreneurial Landscape

There was a time when the barriers to entry for any entrepreneur into any industry were high. Not only were there barriers in terms of knowledge, expertise and experience, but the setup costs and running costs were also very high.

Before the internet when people used to think about setting up a business, this was a major deal. They'd have to consider how they would fund the operation and you couldn't even begin to think about setting up a business if you weren't prepared to put down at least five figures as an investment. Many people didn't entertain the thought of their own business because of this reason alone.

This meant that people were a whole lot more committed to their business and would do everything in their power to make it work because there was a lot more at stake.

Everything about setting up a traditional business was expensive, from fixed running costs to purchasing stock, to paying for advertising in printed media. You had to think through how you were going to produce the service or product you wanted to offer, and this would take time and effort. Even if they had done considerable market research, at some point they would still have to chance the markets and present their solution, which might turn out to be a flop. This of course means you are placing a lot of up front capital for something that may ultimately fail for any number of reasons.

The internet changes all this because it's made it possible for anyone to set up a new business and become successful at low cost with extremely low barriers to entry.

Imagine you were planning on setting up an accountancy practice. In the past you would have to advertise in local newspapers or any other printed media, you'd have to do a lot of business networking in order to meet potential clients, you'd have to get all your paperwork ready and have your services on a flyer or something to hand out to potential customers. You'd need of course to have a business card and all this costs money to set up. Before you've even taken your first customer, there's a considerable investment.

If you wanted to set this up today using the internet as your primary mechanism for business, you could get all your digital paperwork ready (at no cost), you could do a lot of business networking from your bedroom on social media websites and networking websites, you can have a digital flyer created in the form of a website (at no cost, if you went with a DIY solution), and you could have business cards printed for you for an extremely low cost.

You see it suddenly becomes a lot cheaper.

I remember when I tried to set up my first venture in 1997 (which was a ski touring group); I designed some business cards by myself and went to a high street printer to have 200 made up. I remember the cost of that was about £250 and at that time this was a lot of money. I was 1 year into my first job and wasn't earning a great deal, and I was really keen on doing something entrepreneurial.

Firstly the card design was total rubbish, but I thought it looked great at the time! These days you can get 200 printed business cards for around £15 or pay a little more and get fully designed ones. You see the internet has made it cheaper for printers to do business, and that cost saving is passed down to you the customer.

It used to be that if you wanted to sell electronic items, you'd have to have a shop, have the products engineered, designed and made. The products would then need to be branded and packaged before you could send them to your customer, so long as you have an outlet to sell. When you get the products manufactured, you'd also have to do large runs because that's just how things were done back then with the cost of production.

Can you imagine how much money is needed to do that?

You can now do the same thing for a fraction of the cost. Literally you can source a supplier of products ready to be branded, manufactured in China, engineered and ready packed for distribution, for a fraction of the cost. Plus you can do short manufacturing runs to test the market first!

It's amazing to think that all this is possible because of the advanced communications that the internet has brought about. You can see how this opens up the market for the budding entrepreneur and over the last 5-10 years the landscape has shifted considerably. We are living in an age when we can be sitting on a beach in Barbados and checking our sales orders on a mobile device smaller than a classic Mills and Boon novel.

It blows my mind away to think that we can do all of this, yet so few people actually consider the potential power of using the internet for their business. It's a total game changer when you know how to make it work for you.

We can reach people easier and quicker than ever before

Access to the market is right now unparalleled. There has never been a time in history before now when you could simply go online and get access to a customer in another country and make a direct sale to them.

From your computer you can now have a face to face conversation with someone on the other side of the planet; that's profound, when you think about the origins of trade and the origins of the market.

The speed of communication has literally reduced to instantaneous. Barring satellite disruptions or service outages, on a perfect day, you can talk, email, or send an SMS text to someone and they will get it instantly.

This is a crucial component for entrepreneurs because this forms the basis of one of the greatest benefits of a small business entrepreneur and that is being able to act fast on information.

It is far easier for a small business to adapt to new economic or legislative changes than it is for a medium to large organisation. This gives small businesses the first mover advantage. It is important to understand that it's your job as a new business owner to stay on top of the information that is coming to you, because being able to do something about it quicker than big businesses is your unique advantage.

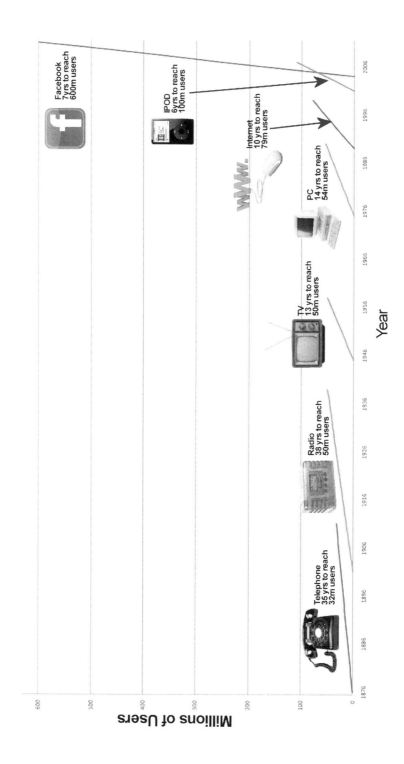

I remember back in 2005 there was a series of new legislations brought out in the USA regarding the legality of online gambling transactions and this affected one of my projects at the time. It meant that we had to change a lot of the advertising systems we were using in order to comply with the new rules. I made this change over the course of a few weeks and the results were that we didn't get hit by the legislation. We were able to adapt and change immediately. Some larger operators were not so fortunate and could not adapt in time before they saw their profits drop and some eventually went out of business.

Think about how eBay has changed the way people purchase retail goods. No longer do people need to walk into a shop and view the items in order to buy goods ranging from the smallest things like pens, notebooks, paperclips, through to large items like cars and even property.

The range of products is nearly infinite and you can find just about anything online. People are selling to each other from all over the world. Chances are if you've bought something on eBay, you've purchased something from the other side of the planet.

As mentioned already, factories are supplying the end user now. If you've not come across Alibaba before, go take a look today. This is a site that connects people with the factories in China and gives people the ability to produce branded goods direct from the manufacturing line.

Recently we had a batch of USB flash drives made up for our company, branded and boxed, and all this at a cost that equates to two pairs of jeans! There is no way that was possible even just 3 years ago.

Social media has increased global connectivity to the point where you can communicate with anyone in the world anytime.

Aggregator and distribution services online have helped to spread people's messages at ever-increasing rates. I sat in a Starbucks in Tokyo a couple of years ago and from my mobile phone I could send a message that was visible to hundreds of people within my network back in the UK.

It's never been easier to setup a complete business

The cost of starting a business is almost zero now. You can have a company registered and trading for as little as £100. There are so many services online that you can use for free that will enable you to produce things, to contact people, to network, to design and build an online store, the possibilities are endless.

Even when I started back in 2001, I managed to set up with a budget of zero, and back then most of these free services did not exist. In fact Facebook and other social media weren't even around and people had only just begun using emails to market.

I remember sitting at my little computer desk each night building my first website and wondering if it would ever make money. It was both frightening and exciting at the same time because I actually felt like I was building something substantial that I could call a business, and I felt totally empowered that I could do it all from a single computer.

We are at a stage in economic development where everybody should consider himself as a factory producing goods or services. People are changing jobs faster and quicker than ever and projects come and go as often as rain in England which means society is moving towards a shifting model of employment where companies will consider short-term contracts more cost effective solutions than hiring for longevity.

We're moving into a society where groups of skilled people come together to complete tasks and then disband to do other things. Even musicians are working like this where bands will stay as a band yet individual band members also have the flexibility to go pursue solo careers.

We are all producers, so what are you producing in your life?

You can set up a business in under 2 hours

It's so fast to get things done. Automated systems online have made it possible to get your business up and running in just a few hours. Isn't that amazing? I know people who have literally woken up one morning and gone to bed with a brand new business ready to roll.

You don't need to be a registered company to start trading, you can simply start and register later. Even so, if you did want to register a company, there are sites where you can do this and within minutes it's all set up with the official paperwork in the post on its way to you.

There are sites where you can create small websites or even places where you can sell your services without your own site. We've already mentioned eBay, however if instead you wanted to sell your services, you can do it via one of many outsourcing websites which connect people looking for project work, to those who can accomplish that work.

Business is more transparent than ever

One of the biggest shifts in business philosophy has been the introduction of increased transparency in company communications internally and externally. For businesses, this means that they are being more open, more communicative and they are holding themselves more accountable. The net results of this means that customers have more information about the way businesses behave.

This means that there is no room for deception and ultimately the customer can find out everything about you whether you choose to reveal that information or not.

With the internet, business is becoming more transparent every day, and every single transaction online is traced and recorded in some digital form. This means there has been a fundamental shift of momentum towards delivering services and products where the true value can be easily understood.

This means that those famous infomercials in the late 80s and 90s that sold people stuff they didn't need and didn't want, are totally out. They've transformed into something else now where they must deliver the true promise of what they are selling.

What this means for new business owners is that all is fair when it comes to selling online. You stand just as much chance of gaining a customer as the next person in your chosen industry, as long as you can show that your offer is of higher value.

Besides delivering something that is of real value to people, you must also make your solution unique in some way. It's a common understanding in starting a business that what you sell must be unique in order to differentiate yourself from your competition.

When I started my first website, our unique aspect in the market place was that we had the best overall design and our technical functionality was always miles above the competition. To this date, that same project is running and that website is still the technically most advanced website in its category.

Here are some questions that might help you to find what is unique about your offer:

- Can your offer be replicated easily?

- Has there been any innovation in your work?

- What makes your product better than the competition?

- How can you add a twist to your service that will give it even more value?

- Is your customer service the same as your competition? If so, why is it? Why not make it miles better?

Filtering out the fraudsters

The internet makes it a lot easier to find who the rogue operators are in your industry. This means customers will very quickly find out who they can trust to purchase from and who not to. The message is spread so quickly that it really doesn't pay to be a fraudster by offering poor and low value services.

One of the biggest areas of growth right now is in internet marketing. Everybody needs it; more and more companies realise the power of the internet and how it can dramatically improve their business.

There is however a lot of what I call the new "Get Rich Quick" schemes of the Noughties.

Please beware of these because there are many people out there who call themselves experts in the field of internet marketing, yet they've had less than a few years' experience and are themselves still in full-time employment. Don't get intoxicated by their seemingly simplistic offer, they'll leave you seeing pink elephants.

Be extremely wary of people telling you they can help you to make five figures in a month by applying just a few hours work a week. I've seen the most ridiculous offers of people teaching you to promote electronic books and making over $100,000 per month doing it. It's just not true, but people still get fooled into buying those systems because they are lazy, they want the results now, and they don't have any good ideas of their own.

If this is you, and at one point you've succumbed to these systems, then it's not too late, you can still create something of true value and learn to deliver something to the internet business world that you can truly be proud of.

I've been in this business for 13 years and I've generated over $10m for our clients and the one thing I'm sure of when it comes to internet marketing is that it works just as traditional marketing works. You must put in the time effort and correct steps in order to get the results you are aiming for.

Over the last 13 years, I've been involved in almost every aspect of internet marketing, from banner advertisements to pay-per-click schemes to affiliate marketing and one thing I know for sure, you have to put the effort in and you must learn and work at the system that will work for you.

In all of my time working with digital business, now is the most dangerous time of all because there are more fraudsters around now than I've ever seen before. It would seem that the con artists are here to stay, so stay diligent and learn what works and what doesn't.

REPEAT AFTER ME - I WILL NOT BE SUCKED IN BY THE FRAUDSTERS SELLING GET RICH QUICK ONLINE SCHEMES!

Provide a bad service and everyone will know

Providing an exceptional customer service experience is absolutely paramount to success online. Due to the impersonal nature of the internet, where people can buy without having to interact with other human beings, customer service becomes even more important because one fault in your automated system will create a terrible customer experience. If you then fail to deliver a fantastic resolution to the problem, people will tell other people about it and the message of your poor service will spread quicker than you can even imagine.

Quite a famous story is that of the sleeping technician from Comcast. Comcast are one of the largest home internet providers in the US and in this story, the customer finds the technician sleeping whilst on support in his home. Not only was the technician sleeping, he was also overheard telephoning the Comcast support helpline to help him fix the problem in the customer's home.

Instead of calling the company, the customer recorded the sleeping technician on video and edited it to include a few funny quotes and then uploaded it to YouTube, still visible today. The video has had 1.6 million views, and the repercussions of this were very bad. The technician got fired straight away and the embarrassment and negative press that Comcast got from this was substantial.

People can find out everything about you online

I've talked about the need to be transparent with online business. Another thing that makes this even more important is that people can find out everything about you online.

For example, I have logs on our website visits and we can trace a single click all the way back to the originator and get their phone number and call them immediately to ask them how they felt the website was for them. That's how detailed the internet tracking is these days.

Besides the technology which is in place to track all your records and record all transactions on a website, there is something also more organic about being able to research people online.

Your online profile must reflect your company brand

A first impression makes a huge difference when it comes to online sales. Because of the plethora of choice online, you literally have seconds to impress.

Most people will not consider themselves as part of their company branding, however with the impersonal nature of the internet, customers are looking for more personality in brands than ever before and one way which customers are gauging this is through personal profiles of the owner.

Owners have to consider that people will research them online and so your message as an owner should be totally congruent with the message of your company.

You need to be absolutely clear about who you are and what your purpose and goals are, such that when a potential customer 'Googles' you, they find exactly what they expect, a message which is true and clear and supports the business vision that you have conveyed on your company literature or website.

If you're thinking one bad impression is not so bad, then consider that it takes seven good impressions to reverse a bad impression. If there is a customer who is on the point of purchasing your services, researches you online and finds that you aren't projecting the same branding as your business, then it would take you seven positive marketing messages to that person before they will even consider your services again.

Position yourself with the right people

With so much social networking at play and photos being shared daily, it's more important than ever to be positioned with the right people.

What this means is that you have to be seen with the influential people in your industry. It raises your own profile and provides some comfort to customers to tell them that they are dealing with the right person. That they are working with a 'mover and shaker'.

Another way to generate position within a market place is to issue press releases about things that are happening with your company, including anything happening within the industry you are in that your company is acting upon.

This gives you massive relevance and your audience will see that you are active on the forefront of your industry.

Eventually the truth is always revealed online

It's simple. I've already discussed the need for transparency and also how incredibly easy it can be to track all your activities. I've also talked about how your profile is publically available. It's the internet, everything is public, nothing is personal.

So the ultimate truth is that the truth about you or your business will always eventually be revealed online in some form.

This means be honest, truthful, delivering high value services and work to your highest ideals. I can't reiterate how important this is. Unfortunately for those who might think that it's easy to con a few people online, it's really the worst move you can make because sooner or later it will backfire with extreme prejudice.

I remember a few years back there was an interesting case of an unscrupulous operator in the affiliate marketing world who was literally selling 'make money online schemes'. The methods and strategies that this operator employed were fairly standard business practices, however it was the intent that made this all the more nasty.

The fact was, she had made up various stories and testimonials and also created fictitious statistics in order to sell a scheme that would teach people how they could also do the same and make lots of money for very little work. Many people were sucked into the hype, however eventually another well-known figure in the industry spoke out about her and literally overnight that rogue operator was shut down, not from regulators cracking down, but from the general public and customer base spreading the word quicker than you can blink an eye.

So what should you do if something did go wrong inadvertently with your company or your product? Well you should be the first to issue a public apology explaining the situation in full so that there is no room for rumours to emerge before you've had your official news released.

So what's the catch?

If being an entrepreneur online were easier than ever, it would sound like there are no real catches, right? You might be thinking right now about all the new ideas in your head and how you can make a business out of them, but before you get carried away there are things you need to consider.

You see, the way business works online is that it's more organic than ever. It's interesting that this should be the case considering that the internet is the largest technological innovation of the century.

The reason it's so organic is because the incredible high level of connectivity that the internet delivers creates something as complex as a set of neural pathways. When something goes incredibly right or incredibly wrong with your online business, you will never be able to determine exactly the reason why because everything is happening at the same time so the cause of a particular outcome is always dependant more than one contributing factor.

It almost comes down to gut feeling based on experience and that's one reason why new internet marketers fail and why experienced internet markets succeed.

So there is a catch. The catch is that in the very early stages of setting up an online business you will find it very hard to determine which actions you take have resulted in the success or failure of your venture. Your best bet is to ensure you take all the right steps and make positive forward movements in all the areas needed, such that you cover all bases and don't put all your efforts into a single channel of marketing online.

Always seek out expertise to consult with and always do what feels right for you.

Workshop 2: Discovering your Values

To get you started on the road to success, let's test your mindset to see if you are thinking about things in the right way.

1. Write down the top five values that are most important to you in relation to the success of your business.

2. For each value, write down in a few short sentences why that value is important in relation to your business. It is important in this part to write in long hand with full flowing sentences.

3. Look out for the following conditions in your sentences:

    a. Negations – any statement which could be deemed negative

    b. Necessity – any statement that implies a state of need or requirement, these are marked by words such as: need, should, must.

    c. Comparisons – any statement that is comparing to the past or to other people/companies.

4. Each of the sentences you've identified in step 3 above are Limiting Decisions. These are disempowering states that do not serve you moving forward.

5. For each sentence, ask yourself the question, "How does this reason help me moving into the future?"

6. Reframe all the negative sentences by reversing them into positive reasons for success.

    a. For example, "I'm dyslexic, I can't possibly succeed", could be reframed as, "Richard Branson was dyslexic and look at what he achieved".

7. Take a look at your top two business role models and ask yourself what you think their top five values are.

8. Without looking at your old values list, ask yourself the question again what your top values are now. Perhaps you've discovered a few new ones; perhaps some of the old ones don't apply anymore.

Congratulations, you've just done some valuable work here and these challenging questions have helped you to identify lots of new mindset challenges that you might not have otherwise discovered.

CHAPTER 2

Notes

SECRET 3

Develop the Mindset

By now I think you've realised that the greatest asset you have in your new online business venture is your mindset. I'm sure you've noticed that a lot of the ideas I suggest are all focused around the mindset component, so it won't be any surprise that I'm going to tell you now that developing your own mindset is the single most important factor to success as an internet entrepreneur.

Mindset is important because everything we do begins as a momentary flash of thoughts in our heads. Everything you see around you, from the lights shining from the light bulbs to the floor underneath your feet, started as a thought in someone's mind.

Technological knowledge is not so important because you can go out and find thousands of web designers or developers. However, we will cover the technicalities and what to look for in a later chapter.

The mindset is without a doubt the most important and even though at the time when I first started I didn't know this, looking back I realise that it was my mindset that really made the difference to my success.

At this stage I'm going to say outright that becoming a successful internet entrepreneur is no different to becoming successful in any given enterprise. You have to have the right mentality to do it. I can't tell you a series of steps and actions to take so that you'll become rich. It just doesn't work like that and anyone out there telling you that they can teach you a system to get rich online, run from them as quick as you can.

The mindset is your thoughts and how they control the actions you take, whether those actions are taken consciously or unconsciously. These can amount to attitudes towards ideas, behaviour patterns and methods or strategies used to implement plans.

Every thought you have about your business will inevitably play into the grand equation of your success. This is why it is so important to work on your mindset before you even begin developing your business system.

Talking about mindset is an entire book in itself, and I'm no expert in psychology or human behaviour, so I'm not going to spend time on this considering you can go out and buy hundreds of books on the topic.

What I am going to do is to relate how it works for internet entrepreneurs and how you can learn, from me and other entrepreneurs, what kind of mindset it takes to succeed online.

Knowing your purpose

Ok, by far the biggest question I'm going to ask of you from this book is the reason why you are embarking on this journey, this path into entrepreneurialism online.

It's often difficult to answer this question of why we do the things we do because a vast majority of times we actually do things we don't intend to do on a conscious level, but we do them as a reaction to deep unconscious fears within us.

I don't know what your reasons are, but the one thing I do know is that you should make them positive, forward thinking with a lot of momentum, and you should constantly remind yourself why you are pursuing this path in life.

This purpose will be your biggest driving force that will bring your online business to success.

There is a bigger reason why this is important

When I first started to develop my websites and online businesses, I never thought there was any other reason than to make money and enjoy more choice and opportunity in life. However, as I continued on the path and now 13 years later, I have learnt enough about myself to know that throughout this whole time, I had greater reasons why I was so driven and these reasons I hold dear in my heart.

These are the reasons you must find for yourself. What your vision is of the world and how you'd like to live in the future will provide you with the will to carry on.

I can't tell you how you'll find those reasons, all I can do is tell you some stories about what drives me and what my bigger reasons are.

As I've mentioned already, helping disadvantaged people is something I've wanted to do on a large scale. I remember there was this one time when I was sitting in a very good friend's house. This was back in 2004 when I was beginning to come into some serious money from my online work.

I had a singular mission back then – all I was interested in was how to make money online. I was extremely passionate about being successful, and I completely believed that it was possible to do it online. When success came my way, I noticed that friends' attitudes towards me would start to change.

There were those who became quite jealous, and then there were those who were still cynical and didn't believe that it was sustainable.

Whilst I was sitting there my friend said to me, "all you seem to be interested in is making money, there's more to life than money you know." I was quite taken back by this; however I could understand from his point of view, all he could see was the actions I was taking, which all pointed to the immediate truth that profit was at that time my primary focus. It's true, profit should be high on your radar because without it, your business would fail.

Any entrepreneur will tell you that profits come first.

I had to explain my motivations because people don't see that side of me. I said to my friend, it wasn't about the money, it was about what the money could do for me in terms of opportunities and choices. It was here that I said I wanted to be able to give more than just £5 a month to charity, and to be able to one day give a charity £1m and together we would really help some people.

This was one of my big reasons why it was important for me to succeed; however unknown to me at the time, there was an even bigger reason why this was so important, a reason that came to light when I began to look at my life in greater detail.

Back in 2001 I had a couple of good female friends whom I was very close to and within a 9-month period, both came to me with horrific stories of what had happened to them. I'm a very trustworthy person and a lot of my friends knew this, so quite often friends tell me things that they wouldn't tell other people because they know I can be trusted.

What I didn't expect was the terrible things that they told me about, how they had suffered in their lives and continued to suffer physical and sexual abuse in the form of blackmail and rape. It was harrowing to hear these stories; being a sensitive person, I really felt awful and wanted to do something about it. One girl had even had a gun pointed to her head whilst the physical rape happened and the other one still had ongoing situations at work where her boss was literally forcing himself on her. I told her to tell the police about it, but she decided not to in the end. It's such a sensitive topic because for some women they don't even want to acknowledge that it happened.

I thought to myself how could any man be so terrible, how could people end up in these situations and I was ready to fight someone each time they spoke to me about it.

In 2001 I was not a confident man. There were many things that I was good at, however standing up for myself, let alone other people, was not something I could do with any great effect. These stories shook me to my very core as I felt powerless to help and I felt disgusted that any man on this planet could think that this was acceptable behaviour when women are literally the bearers of our species.

I decided then unconsciously that if there ever was a day when I could do something about it I would. I decided that in order to create the choices, and to be able to do something about it for other people, I would need to make a lot of money to make a big difference.

This was my deep core reason for becoming an entrepreneur, the need to help people in need. I hope that this has given you some insight as to what drives us as human beings. I like to think that I'll leave this planet in a better place than when I came into it. What will you do to help our planet?

Create the future you want for yourself

I've mentioned already about visualizing as a process that greatly helps your mindset to get what it is you're trying to do.

To elaborate on this, remember I said that your mind cannot tell the difference between a real and an imagined thought. This is one of the pinnacles, in my mind, of successful entrepreneurs.

When you were a child, you would have wanted to be someone when you grew up. Often parents will ask their children this question and some typical answers include cowboy, fireman, astronaut, princess etc.

Think about this, when you answered that question as a child, did you have any doubt whatsoever whether it was impossible or not? Of course not, in your mind as a child, you absolutely believed that it was going to happen.

It's only until you start growing up that the environment around you starts to place negative doubts in your head as to what is possible.

Anything is possible, you just have to want it enough.

So what do you want for your future in your life? How do you see yourself living 5 years from now and what would you like to be doing? Perhaps you want to be living in a bigger house with an indoor swimming pool, or maybe you'd like to be checking up on your sales from your beach house?

Gandhi wanted a free India, democratic and peaceful; he said, "You must be the change you want to see in the world." He lived his life according to how he saw the future to be and through his absolute conviction he achieved what everybody thought was impossible.

I want you to be the change you want to see in your life.

If you were successful 5 years from now and living a dream life, how would you behave, how would your attitudes have changed and wouldn't you be more confident? So be all of that now and begin to feel successful today. After all, how many people embark on an exciting adventure on entrepreneurialism that could shape their life for the better?

Keep your drive on fire

When you have all your reasons, both the materialistic and the idealistic, you must keep reminding yourself of them. These are the aspirations and goals you've set yourself, so keep your eye on the target.

It's ok if from time to time you get a little diverted from them, so long as they are visible and clear and you get back on course. There are many routes to get from A to B, even a sat nav will keep recalculating the best route when you take a diversion from its suggested route. The key is always to keep the destination in mind and your actions will move towards it eventually.

Visual visualisation

I love this idea of keeping your goals visual. I've kept vision boards, vision cards and vision journals in my time and right now my favourite is the vision journal.

Ok, if you've never come across these before then there's no better time to start than now. These are simply a collection of images or words that remind you of your goals, collected and organised in either a board, cards or journal format.

The way I think about it, it's kind of like when you were a child, you would cut out images of the things you wanted in life. When you grew older and became a teenager, you would have posters of the celebrities you wanted to be when you grew up!

The principle is the same; it's all about reminding yourself visually of what you want. This is an extremely powerful yet simple technique.

Get yourself a cork pin board and cut out images of your goals and pin them on. Keep this board in visual range so you can see it all the time somewhere near your work.

Another way of doing it is getting these images in business card size and laminating them. Then you can carry some with you in your wallet whenever you want.

My favourite though so far has been using my vision journal. I loved the idea of a visual diary so much I created a platform for recording one's own video diaries.

Visit www.mindlogr.com to create your own video diary for tracking your progress.

Essentially it is a photo album where I can easily add and remove pictures, and I've created categories within the album. My first three categories in the album are Vision, Purpose and Mission. I've filled these pages up with images and words that remind me what these are for me.

Many people have different definitions of these three ideas, here are mine.

Vision is how I would like to see the world and how I would like to see my life in some ideal version of it in the future.

Purpose is the reasons why I have the vision that I have, and the reasons that drive me towards it.

The Mission is how I'm going to go about getting there. These aren't specific strategies like I'm going to get there by making more money online. These are more mindset hows, like I'm going to act more confidently to ensure my message is transmitted across more effectively.

Further pages in the album contain other categories of interest for me, these may be different for you, but generally it's what's important to you. I have things like wealth, health, family, relationships, luxury items, home, and charity.

Why I like the journal is because whenever I want to go look at it, it is a very purposeful action on my part to pick up the journal and review the pages. It's the intent in my mind that I want to be reminded, and that to me is more effective for me.

Find the method that works for you and use it.

Writing journals

I can't stress enough how important it is to write your thoughts down on paper. This is another great way to keep that drive moving forward.

I highly recommend taking pen to paper and not typing your journal. When you write with a pen, your brain has to activate a whole different set of neural pathways in order to control your fingers to write the words you are thinking. This process shifts the modality in which your mind thinks about whatever you are writing; in our case, here, it's about business. This translation of modality from pure thought to intended action on the part of your writing gives great force and clarity to what you are saying.

It's a great way to reflect each day on what you've done and what you're intending to achieve. When you start to let the words flow, you'll sometimes find it consoling to voice your concerns; often you'll also find resolutions to your own problems. It's an empowering process that I highly recommend. It only takes 5-10 minutes to write a single page, and the benefits are massive.

Accountability by proxy

This method is not one for the frail minded, however it can be an incredible driving force if you have the right friends who can support you in your endeavours.

Essentially, this is telling your closest friends about your intended plans and asking them to support and challenge you the whole time. It's not ok for them just to support you unconditionally because that is unrealistic.

We've all had friends who wanted to be musicians and, at their early gigs, the audience was always their best friends and friends of friends and guess what, the feedback was always positive! That doesn't really help because we all know there's something we need to improve or change to be better, so the best advice is the honest advice.

Why do you think Simon Cowell is so successful at what he does? It's because he tells it like it is!

Ask your friends to tell you like it is, have them criticise you, challenge your ideas and get them to keep you on your toes. This can serve you incredibly well because it will make you accountable to not only yourself, but also to your best friends and family.

One of my own best critics was always my mother. She would never believe that it would work and every time she pointed out something that might not work, I set out to improve, change or just make it work. I was accountable to her, just as much as I was to the charities I wanted to help.

I just wanted to prove to everyone that it would work and it was possible to become financially free with an online business. In 2004, that dream became a reality and I've never looked back since.

Discipline yourself as if you were the naughty child in your family

Taking action is the number one thing that leads to the success of so many new business ventures. Too many new entrepreneurs fail to act or take the right action. Those who just talk and don't do will eventually talk themselves out of success.

Get off your backside

When I think about getting off your backside and taking action there's only one person that comes to mind and that is of an inspirational man called Sean Stephenson. There's no one better to spread the word about taking action and making things happen by acting.

Sean is 3ft tall, told he was going to die at birth because he has a rare bone disorder which leaves him confined to a wheelchair, which for most people would mean leading an insignificant life. However for Sean, he's lived life taking positive action all the time and now he's written a book called *Get off your But*, a book about the excuses we give ourselves which stop us from taking action.

In his time he has work on Capitol Hill and in the White House as Presidential Liaison for the office of Cabinet Affairs. He's started his own speaking company, sharing the stage with Tony Robbins and Mark Victor Hanson. He's also received board certification in Clinical Psychology and is currently doing his PhD at American Pacific University.

He is a shining example of how anything is possible regardless of what other people think. The little man is a legend in my mind and has the mindset of a champion. I had the greatest pleasure to meet him in 2009 and I won't forget the impact it had on me to see someone so frail, make such a huge impact in the planet.

Last year's intentions

A way I like to see how much action I've taken is to review the previous year and to think about what I wanted to achieve at the beginning of the year, versus what I actually managed to achieve.

It helps if you create yearly plans, then you can look back at those plans to see how much of it you've actually done.

If you want to test yourself, think about what you wanted to do last year and then give yourself a percentage of how much of it you really did.

I look back at 2010 at one project in particular and noticed that I didn't do everything I wanted to there, but I did do almost 80% of it. Again I think it comes down to the 80/20 rule. By checking back I can tell that I did take a lot of action and so even if those were the wrong actions to take, at least I made some forward movement.

Become a Master by being disciplined and persistent

The gurus and masters of the ancient worlds never just became them overnight. They had to work hard and long and for the most part to strict rules in order to achieve their status as masters.

Martial arts are a great example of how discipline over time breeds experience, skill and mastery of your art. Malcolm Gladwell in his book *Outliers* talks about the 10,000 hour rule which is the average number of hours someone needs to achieve mastery in their skill.

Becoming an internet entrepreneur takes a lot of skill and patience as well as discipline to keep going when things are looking tough.

I've learnt various forms of martial arts since I was young and for all those lessons and times I do remember that the discipline I learnt has been invaluable to me. I know at times things are tough and it is during these times when absolute faith and belief must prevail in order to get through and succeed.

Thinking about the 10,000 hours that Gladwell talks about always reminds me of the first 3 years of my own enterprise and how, during this time, the sum total of what I made in profits amounted to Big Mac and fries. I could have given up at any point during those 3 years, but the discipline I had in maintaining momentum and also being focused to learn as much as possible without giving up really helped me through those tough times.

Sometimes in order to succeed you must be prepared to go above and beyond those boundaries that hold us back. I toiled day and night and eventually my efforts paid off. I became a master of my trade and in the early days it was in website design and search engine optimisation.

If you wanted examples of success through discipline then you need look no further than stories from the world of magic. Magicians are incredibly talented and incredibly disciplined people. The extremely high degree of complexity of magic tricks and illusions often require years of practice to get right.

Harry Houdini was one of the most sensational of them all, first starting out doing card tricks, he eventually specialised in escape acts. He first started out as 'The Handcuff King', specialising in handcuff escapes and eventually moved onto more daring acts of escape which include the Chinese water torture cell and the suspended straightjacket escape.

His dedication to his art was second to none, as he constantly kept innovating new escape acts when his acts started to get imitators. Each time he created a new act he would have to spend a lot of time in practice to ensure that every nuance of the act was accounted for. His discipline in this was known throughout the magic world and quite rightly so because any oversight could have cost him his life.

In this story we can all learn than discipline can be both the factor that creates success, or it could also be the factor that creates failure if it is not sufficiently practiced.

The other trait that I've found must be developed is the attitude of total persistence. Besides being disciplined over the first 3 years of my business, I also had to persist and keep going no matter what.

In Napoleon Hill's book *Think and Grow Rich*, which I would highly recommend you read, his chapter on persistence defines it as, "... an essential factor in the procedure of transmuting desire into its monetary equivalent. The basis of persistence is the power of will."

Something I heard Will Smith say in a YouTube video I watched quite recently sums up the attitude you must have. He said, "If you and I stepped onto a treadmill, I'd die before I got off." It's the attitude that you would never give up, no matter what.

For me, the definition of persistence I like to adopt is not taking no for an answer. Henry Ford is another great story about how he persisted with his engineers to get them to build the first eight-cylinder engine cast in one single block. Often regarded as ruthless, Henry Ford would never take no for an answer and armed with the designs on paper, he instructed his team to build the engine.

His team reportedly complained, issuing remarks that it was impossible, but Ford persisted and told them it didn't matter how much time it would take. The engineers had no choice but to continue if they wanted to keep their jobs. Six months went by, then another six months and the engineers kept saying it was impossible, yet Ford persisted saying, "I want it, and I'll have it." At the end of the year, by some feat of engineering, the engine was finally cast making Ford the superpower in the car industry it is today.

The mindset of a successful entrepreneur

There's one thing that makes the difference between an entrepreneur and a successful entrepreneur – the mindset that the successful entrepreneur has managed to develop.

Whether that is through a lot of learning by induction, or whether that is purposeful learning, in both cases, it had to be learned. Entrepreneurs weren't just born with that tendency to succeed, they had to have learnt it somewhere.

There are some entrepreneurs who've learnt a lot of lessons from their parents, sometimes being around people we begin to adapt and learn those behaviours. It's obvious when you think about it, even people who've been in an organisation long enough will begin to adapt to their way of working, their rules, behaviours and even speech patterns.

In much the same way, many successful entrepreneurs learnt from their environment as children. Donald Trump is a great example. He has in countless interviews mentioned all the things he had learnt from his father, simply by being around him and hearing him speak on the phone.

The point I'm making is that anything can be learnt, from a language through to a specific attitude or behaviour that cultivates success.

One thing I certainly learnt from my parents was tenacity and putting in the hard work. I would think back to those times when I was literally typing away at my computer designing my first website and thinking to myself that all that hard work would pay off in the end. This is much like the same attitude my parents had when they first moved to the UK from Hong Kong. They worked long and hard hours and I would remember that they always said that the hard work would pay off in the end. They had the belief and strength to know that what they did was going to pay off and they never lost sight of that target.

So how do successful entrepreneurs think about start-up ventures?

When I think about how many successful entrepreneurs started, and I consider the kind of mental attitude I had myself, it came down to three core thoughts that I think propels someone to become good at what they do.

Act, Act, Act

The first and I think the most important thing is the ability to take action. It sounds simple enough, all you have to do is to take action. However, having spent some time with other new business owners, looking and speaking to those who succeed and those who fail, there is one constant I've always come across: those who succeed take massive action.

It doesn't matter if that is the wrong action because there is always something to be learned from it all. In fact some of our greatest lessons and developments as people and as a business are through taking the wrong action. After all, how do we know what's good or bad without having a basis of comparison?

Taking action is so important I just have to keep telling you this! I would have to say that from my experience, out of the people who say they want to do something with an online business, less than 5% actually act on it, and that is a sad statistic indeed.

I often wonder what it is that stops people from acting and I think mostly it comes down to fears. Possibly fear of failure or even more likely a whole heap of limiting beliefs that serve to create inaction.

I don't have the time.
I don't have the skill set.
I don't have enough capital.
I haven't got the contacts.

Whatever those limitations are, they are only there if you put them there. You can reframe these to your advantage, so instead of the thoughts above, why not replace them with these:

I have just as much time as everyone else on the planet; it's not about how much time I have, it's about what I do with the time that matters. I don't have the skill now, but I can learn it or have someone teach me. I don't need capital to get started, it's all about value, so what value have I got which can be exchanged for services that I need to get started? It doesn't matter that I don't have the contacts, there are lots of free networking opportunities out there, so all I have to do is turn up.

Anything that you tell yourself can be changed to work for you, rather than against you.

STOP READING RIGHT NOW, and go take some positive action towards your new online business.

Failing upwards
So I've hammered home the point about taking action - well at least I hope I have. I'm sure that the inspired action you've just taken has given you even more momentum to move forward in creating your new financially free life.

Remember I said that it doesn't matter what action you take and many times it will be the wrong action leading to failure. Great entrepreneurs make loads of mistakes, because it's these mistakes that show them how not to do it, and get's them closer to how to do it even better. In fact it was James Joyce who said, "Mistakes are the portals of discovery."

This seems to be something I've learnt and observed from successful people and that is that they really don't care about failure, and they don't even think of it as failing. They simply think of it as not the right way of doing and they start again, next time taking the new lessons they've learnt.

This is what I'd like to call Failing Upwards because each time you fail you actually get closer to your end goal. Even if you didn't learn anything from your failure consciously, you would have learnt a lot unconsciously. It might be that you've learnt that you are more tenacious than you thought. Or perhaps you are quite good at finding the flaws in your own idea, which is a great thing because then we can constantly improve. It's worse if you can't find flaws.

It was Thomas Edison himself, inventor of the light bulb who said, *"I have not failed 700 times. I have not failed once. I have succeeded in proving that those 700 ways will not work. When I have eliminated the ways that will not work, I will find the way that will work."*

Another great entrepreneurial story is that of Kentucky Fried Chicken and Colonel Sanders whose recipe was turned down over a reported 1000 times from people who thought it was a poor investment. He didn't stop though and eventually won the investment he required and as we all know, today it's a global brand.

Like most entrepreneurs, I've also had failures and I remember the first venture I embarked on was trying to set up a ski touring group with the aim of taking groups of friends from the UK to ski resorts and showing them a good time. There were so many flaws in the idea but I was fresh and just had a passion for skiing that I wanted to share with everyone else.

Everything I did was doomed to failure, from the business cards without telephone numbers to the website which didn't work. Even with the massive number of operational failures I still managed to take a couple of groups of around 20 people to France and back. It just goes to show what a little passion can achieve.

I remember going to my accountant in 2004 with my current business and hearing him say that he was surprised I'd be back after my ridiculous idea back in 1998. Even though I had failed in my first idea, it didn't stop me from trying something new.

To this day, I still have business ideas that we often try and for the most part fail, but each time I learn something more important and that helps our existing revenue-generating projects to thrive and grow even better.

Do whatever it takes

The third mindset component to adopt is the idea that you'll do whatever it takes to succeed. Now there is of course a caveat to this and that is that you must do only so much as it is ethically and morally safe for you, for your friends and family and for the planet.

That being said, the most keen and eager of entrepreneurs are always prepared to take that one step more than the competition and that is one of the single markers of true passion that I've seen in all enterprising individuals.

If there are things you aren't prepared to do in order to pursue your business dreams of becoming financially free, then you must ask yourself why you're not prepared and also ask yourself, what would happen if you didn't do it?

I don't like to use the word sacrifice, but we've all had to make choices and decisions in life that involved putting something else to one side whilst you focus on something; there's plenty of evidence to show that the most successful have had to make this choice at some time in their business enterprise.

The best case of this lies with Richard Branson who made one of the biggest choices of his entrepreneurial career when he sold Virgin Records, his lifelong passion and first massive success, for a reported $1bn in order to fund Virgin Atlantic Airways, which at the time was coming under increasing competitive pressure from British Airways.

In this story there are two examples of doing whatever it takes, one from Branson making the noble sacrifice for the greater good of the organisation, and then that of British Airways doing whatever it takes to eliminate the competition. It was the so called 'dirty tricks' campaign from British Airways that really showed how far some people were willing to go in order to win.

In my own experience, the choices I've had to make to succeed involved my personal life. In fact, when I first started on my journey back in 2001, I remember clearly saying to myself that I was prepared to sacrifice my entire social life in order to spend that time working and making it successful. I literally worked day and night, and for 3 years I pressed on, hardly socialising or seeing my friends and family. I poured every ounce of energy I had into making it work and eventually it paid off.

I'm not saying that you need to do this as well, I'm just pointing out that you will be faced with some big choices that will confront you to your deepest core and it's those times when you'll know if you are prepared to do what it takes to succeed.

It's not a matter of resources, it's only a matter of Resourcefulness

Entrepreneurs are extremely resourceful people; they always adopt the mindset that there are more than enough resources in the world to do what they need, be it financial resources, materials or whatever.

It's never a case of having enough of the resource, it's always about how to gain access to it. There's a saying, "Where there's a will there's a way," and that's true. I always believe that clichés exist for a reason and that is that they've been said enough by those who believe in them, to make it to cliché-dom.

This is the part where lateral thinking will always help to get around the resource issues you might face when you are starting up in business. A classic story I like to tell people when they complain about resources is another Richard Branson story, which he recounts in his book *Business Stripped Bare*.

Branson gets stuck in an airport due to cancellations and instead of waiting like most people do, he takes his frustration and goes to the other side of the airport where he charters a plane to his destination. However, he didn't have the money to do it, so he makes a cardboard sign selling seats on his charter flight, heads back to the first ticket counter and starts enlisting stranded passengers.

Problem solved. Several writers have hinted that this was the inception of Virgin Airways, though there isn't evidence to show it. Nonetheless, it just shows how fast thinking, gutsy choices and decisions can lead to new ideas and solve a problem. In this story, Branson didn't have the financial resources to charter the plane, so he figured out how he could access the resources.

In my own story on a much smaller scale, I also started my business back in 2001 with no money. In fact I was in quite a lot of debt at the time but I needed services to help me build my first website. I already had a computer and the software, I just needed the web hosting and domain registration, so I asked for a favour from an old college friend of mine who had a small business in web hosting.

I made a promise to myself that I would pay him back the day I made money. I was also lacking knowledge, so I borrowed books from libraries and also spent a lot of time online learning what I needed to, all from free resources.

I knew that the resources were out there and all I had to do was work out how I could get access to them. In the end when I began to make serious money in 2004, I wrote a cheque back to my friend for the whole 3 years' worth with a bonus too. I also believe in karma, some people call it the law of reciprocity, some call it the law of attraction, whatever you know it by, if you do good, you will get it back in multiples.

Entrepreneurs don't take risks

It's a common perception amongst society that entrepreneurs generally have this image of being risk takers. It seems people find solace in being able to explain away massive success by saying that entrepreneurs take huge risks that generally normal people wouldn't take.

In fact new business owners will adopt this belief too and sometimes take unnecessary risk in their start-up venture because they believe they need to.

This is totally incorrect, in fact entrepreneurs make the safest decisions most of the time. You don't think Branson would just sell Virgin Records to fund Virgin Atlantic just on a risky gut feel move.

What seems risky to you, are merely well thought out decisions by entrepreneurs.

I don't know of one entrepreneur, be it online or offline who makes rash risky decisions in the hope of some great reward for being so courageous. All their decisions are based on facts and figures, and this is something that I think must be learnt quite early on to avoid early failure, which often times leads to quick retreat from the entrepreneurial world.

Facts and figures, that scares a lot of people and to be honest I was also not a great fan of statistics, but I did understand that with them I could make better-informed decisions. You must also start collecting statistical data about everything you do. Online, it's all about the stats, from web traffic statistics, to financial data. Use Google Analytics, it's a treasure trove of information waiting for you to analyse and use to your advantage.

Exercise your own personal faith

Faith can mean many things to many different people across the planet. In its shortest form it can be defined as the confident belief or trust in the truth or trustworthiness of a person, concept or thing. In our world there is a distinct lack of faith in oneself these days and in a society where so much value is placed on external acceptance, people have developed the need for other people to believe in them before they believe in themselves.

Take for example many of the reality TV shows that are present today, in particular the music talent shows that allow the general public to compete for a recording contract. How many times have we seen people who make it to the television finals being totally unconfident of themselves? Even after weeks and weeks of practice, getting through the many rounds, they still have a certain disbelief in their own talent.

What makes this worse is that this attitude is somewhat celebrated and wins the approval of people. It's commonly known as supporting the underdog but I see it as an unconscious vicious circle within society that propagates this attitude as the way to be, or even the way to succeed.

This is far from how things actually work; it's unfortunate that the massive impact which mass media has on people has driven this message too far, in my opinion.

I say this because it's absolutely vital for all successful entrepreneurs to have total belief, confidence and conviction in themselves, their ideas and their methods.

The power of self belief is extremely important and I can't stress it enough. There are countless books on the topic, so I suggest you read some of those if you need help in this area.

This isn't just a passing way to say you do believe in yourself, it doesn't need to be verbalised, it's shown in the action and attitude that you take towards your new business venture.

That same story I've already told about Henry Ford being totally persistent when building the engine also shows what incredible belief he had in himself, in the engineers and in the science behind the engineering. It was as if he knew it was going to work, and that's the ultimate attitude to have. Acting like you knew what you were doing was certainly going to succeed.

Gandhi had total belief in a democratic self-governing India; he made that happen despite the many challenges he had along the way.

In my own personal story, during those first 3 years I had no real concept of what my targets were; however I didn't stop believing that it was totally possible to earn a living online and become financially free. I had seen other people do it and personally met many of them, so I had an unwavering belief that if they could do it, then so could I.

I also believed later in year 4 that I could hit a target of £10,000 per month from passive income via the internet, and when I set that target in the summer of 2004, I remember that by being focused and believing that it was going to happen it drove me forward like never before. I hit that target by February 2005.

There's one thing I've learnt about belief and how to develop it in yourself, it's that until you actually meet people who are in a position where you want to be, somehow you don't really believe it to be possible.

I think a lot of the time we hold successful people in some sort of high regard as if they were 'gifted' or 'special' in a way that we could never be, and for the most part when you actually get to meet them in person and chat, you realise that they are just normal people. I believe something powerful happens when you have this realisation that they are 'normal' people like you; I think that is when you begin to believe that it's possible for you too.

If there's one thing I would recommend doing a lot of, it's networking, talking to successful people and finding a way to socialise or conference with those who are in a higher position in the industry you are in. It's best if you can get to meet the gurus of your industry. I guarantee to you that when you have this realisation that you can do it too, you'll know for certain and you'll have the most amazing feelings and thoughts run throughout your entire body.

Assumption is the mother of all f***-ups

I'm going to start by saying that not all assumptions are bad, there are many great ways to utilise assumptions to empower yourself. However in the context of starting a new venture for a new entrepreneur, assumptions are extremely dangerous territory.

Assumptions, also known as presuppositions, exist in language at every level. They're part of the very fabric and nature of the way we talk. For example, when I say something like, "You can buy anything from eBay today," there are many assumptions in such a simple phrase.

I'm assuming you know how to buy, I'm also assuming you have a PayPal account, I'm assuming you have an internet connection and the list could go on. What I'm illustrating here is how our language has all these in-built meanings that could trip someone up.

I'm always coaching my team to make no assumptions when it comes to business. I've found that on the whole, from talking to many business owners, that much of the time the assumptions they make are massively disempowering and often lead to the failure of projects.

I take this attitude on board because I've spent a lot of time reading and studying the biographies of successful global entrepreneurs and one trait I've definitely discovered is that these successful people, this elite group of achievers, will almost always make all their decisions based on fact and statistics.

You might be thinking, of course someone like Donald Trump makes the most rigid factual-based decisions when he's dealing with multimillion dollar deals, I'm sure I can be a little more flexible myself when it comes to my small business. That's an awful way of thinking. Imagine what your business might look like in 3 years time if you were to continue running it based on assumptions – does it even exist?

Whatever level you are at right now, your decisions are more important than ever because your business needs the best possible decisions you can make in order to succeed. If you fail, you'll have to start all over again and that's an extremely hard task for anyone.

Leave nothing to chance or assumption and make the right decision based on facts every time.

Workshop 3: Vision, Purpose and Mission

Spend the next 30 minutes writing your Vision, Purpose and Mission statements, take 10 minutes on each section.

Remember:

- Your Vision is your big picture outcome

- Your Purpose is why you want to achieve this outcome

- Your Mission is how you are going to achieve these goals

Resources exercise

1) List the resources you currently have available to you. List them in the following categories:

    a. Financial help

    b. Friends with useful services

    c. People you know who have large networks

    d. People who have technical knowledge to help you.

2) Write down a list of three things that you can do for these people now that would offer them great value.

Assumption exercises

1) What are you currently assuming about your new start-up business? Write down a complete list of things you are assuming about everything to do with your new business idea.

    a. With each assumption, ask yourself:

        i. Is this a valid assumption? If not, how can I prove it?

        ii. What needs to be done to change this assumption into a fact?

Bonus Mindset Exercises

1) Who can you be accountable to? If you can write a list of three people who can hold you accountable to your goals in business, you should go and contact them and ask them to do so.

2) What limits do you believe you currently have? For each limitation, fully consider each of these questions and do not move on until you have a clear answer:

    a. When did you decide that you had this limitation? Think back to that time when you first made this decision. Whether you were consciously or unconsciously aware, a decision was made.

    b. Where were you when you were deciding that?

    c. ...And just before that moment, where were you?

    d. Now, as you think about your new business venture, notice how many actual options you have now.

    e. Now consider a future where that old decision might have hindered you, and just notice the resources you actually have now.

Notes

SECRET 4

Customers Drive Society

The online customer is in a unique position. Never before has the customer had so much choice at the press of a button. The customer now has the choice where and when they buy, and at what price.

There is literally more choice than the customer can handle, so it's more important than ever to gear your business entirely for the customers' expectations and deliver real value.

One motto I like to live by is always over deliver. This means always giving a little bit more than the customer expects from your product or service. In fact most times we give them something a little bit extra so they are surprised and we deliver that wow factor. For example, when we deliver our service for social bookmarking, we'll always deliver more than the agreed amount, just because we can.

There are a few factors to bear in mind when you think about the customer in relation to an online business and these are covered in this chapter.

The customer has more choice than ever

The unparalleled access to suppliers via the internet is at a point in time that the world has never seen. We are moving towards a society where services that act as a middle man are soon phasing out of existence because the middle man has become the internet.

No longer do we need facilitators to help us to network and do business because there are so many free services online which cover all of this. Think about it for a second, even just a few years ago if you wanted to manufacture goods, you'd have to fly to China, hire a translator and find the right connectors to get you the introduction to the factory owners. Then you'd have to contend with making sure you do business in the right way and respect the culture and traditions of the country.

Now this process has been simplified to such an extent that you can do all of that through a website called Alibaba which is totally free to use. In a fundamental paradigm shift, now the customer has complete control.

This means the way you define your product or service has to be entirely unique. I've already discussed the importance of having a unique idea, so here I'm going to dive into a little bit more depth on niches and micro-niches.

The big question people will ask is what makes your solution better or more unique than the competition, such that I would choose to do business with you?

Let's look at this from a different point of view. Ultimately everyone is selling a solution to a problem. No matter what kind of service or product you create, it is a solution to a problem.

A cup is a solution to the problem of how to hold liquid for consumption. A pen is a solution for the problem of how to write. A TV is a solution to view live video broadcasts. Everything is a solution to a problem.

In the end, the resolution to the problem delivers happiness in some form or another. So what we are really selling is happiness.

If we now look at it from the point of view of happiness, ask yourself what makes your product or service unique in a way that would deliver greater happiness to your end customer. This is the highest value that your solution should aim to fulfil to some degree. If you can identify the elements that will help your solution to do this effectively, you will go a long way in becoming highly competitive in your niche.

When I think about delivering happiness, one example comes straight to mind and that is the company called Zappos.com, which is an online retailer of apparel in the USA. Zappos is a billion dollar company that, in 2009, was sold to Amazon for $1.2bn. I had the privilege of chatting briefly to the CEO Tony Hsieh at a conference in Calgary a couple of years ago and what struck me was how simple his message was. The core value and message of Zappos is 'Delivering Happiness'.

Originally they started out selling shoes in 1999 and were barely making any revenue. Under his leadership, at that time Tony was 24 years old, he took the company from breaking even to grossing over $1bn in 2009.

What he did which was so unique was that from the moment he joined, he made customer service the number one priority to a standard which had never been seen before. This ultimately made customers more than happy; it made them raving fanatics about the company and that then passed onto their employees whom are also raving fans because it's such a great place to work.

It's just a quick example of driving business through core values, an example that shows how delivering it can make a difference.

How do you make your offer unique?

There are lots of ways to be unique, but not all of them will actually give your customers the feeling of value and happiness.

The number one way I like to suggest is to be the best in something. If you are the best in something, then there's no way you would fail. The best in something always has a market.

Think about it, the best legal firm is always in business, the cake shop with the best cakes is always in business, the online retailer with the best returns policy will always be in business, the technology company with the best innovations will always be in business.

So ask yourself this question, how can you make your solution the best solution in some area of your market?

When I started back in 2001 with my first website project, the one thing I knew I could be better at than everyone else in that industry was to make that website the most attractive and more technically advanced than other competing websites. Since then we've moved on and we retain our technical advantage with that particular website by keeping it as the most technical casino portal on the internet.

Be the best in something, and your business will succeed.

You must define the value you are offering

As well as being unique, you must also be clear about the value you are offering to the end customer. Value is often a difficult notion to quantify, however it is ultimately what sells and what you are selling to.

The value offering is often the same as the benefits of the product or service you are delivering. In this you must be clear about what the benefits are. If you cannot find any tangible benefits to your idea, then you must look deeper and find out what it is you are truly selling.

The reason why you have to be clear is that you need to convey this benefit to the customer such that they understand how your service relates to their problem and how they can get value from your service or product.

The responsibility for value always lies with the end customer.

When a customer goes into a shop to buy a hammer, the customer is buying a tool to solve the problem of hitting a nail into something.

The hammer by itself has no value other than the materials it's made of; it's up to the customer to use the hammer efficiently and effectively to get the value the hammer is designed to deliver. Perhaps the hammer has a special grip to enable a better hitting motion; this is a benefit that must be conveyed otherwise the customer may not know to hold the hammer in a special way.

That's just an example; however, you can apply this same way of thinking to any solution.

Always consider how your customers are going to get maximum impact on their problem by using your solution, and how you are going to relay this message to them.

Develop what your brand stands for

In a market place of infinite choice, brand is now more important than ever. The messages that you are sending out through your value offering and your uniqueness will become integrated with some of your brand messages.

Online you must develop your brand to stand out against the rest, so that when hard times come, the customers will always revert to buying the brands because of what they stand for. This has been proven time and time again.

Recently I was at a meeting where Richard Reed, one of the founders of Innocent the drinks company, spoke about a story in the history of Innocent, and how another big drinks company used some guerrilla marketing tactics to enter into the same market.

This other company used nasty tactics like paying shop owners to take Innocent off their shelves. There was an aggressive campaign over a period of time but eventually Innocent won due to its strong branding and more importantly the message the brand stood for. In a real life David versus Goliath story, that other drinks company pulled out of the chilled fruit juice market.

Another great example of branding winning the battle was the advent of mp3 players and the rise of Apple as the dominant force in this. For a time the number one provider of personal music devices was Sony, and in fact most people were looking towards Sony to make the best mp3 player when they first came about, however Apple came along and changed the course of its own history by creating a product that was so compelling that there simply was no competition.

Apple introduced the iPod, a device which had two value offers, it was simple to use, and it was cool.

To this date, all their products live by these 2 value offers, to be simple and to be cool.

Yet another example of branding winning the competition battle is the example of Coca Cola vs. Pepsi debate. Countless books and websites have already stated that in all blind taste tests around the world, Pepsi is always chosen as the better tasting drink, however in the actual market place, Coca Cola is the most dominant brand in the cola drinks market.

This is achieved purely through branding.

The internet is timeless, customers buy anytime they choose

You can't possibly know when a customer makes that final decision when to buy, so from your perspective as an online retailer, you should consider and build your website with the understanding that the customer can choose at ANY time.

All you can do is to make a compelling offer and incentivise people to buy sooner rather than later.

Even if you did know the exact moment in your selling strategy when a customer buys, you've still got an international customer base, which means you still need to account for 24 hour operations.

It's important that you develop strategies to let the customer know that you are still taking care of things even though you are in a different time zone or different place altogether. The customer needs to feel like they are being looked after.

There are two ways you can go about doing this, you can inform the customer about your online working hours, like a shop, or you can set yourself up with enough systemized processes to enable a near-to-24hr system.

The latter is far more complex to integrate and consider, but also has the potential to make the difference in your overall online business strategy. My recommendation for start-ups is to concentrate on a local area first where you can serve and grow from. Casting too wide a net at the beginning will always lead to failure of the business.

Developing communications and rapport online

Because the internet is timeless, it's vital to develop and maintain rapport with your customers at all time. It's quite tricky to build rapport online because so much of rapport is based around human interaction; however there are many ways to start a business relationship even though you are not physically present.

One of my favourite ways to develop that business relationship is to use online video. Since the inception of video into online media, the format has exploded rapidly with YouTube being a massive success and now it is the second most used search engine in the world. This statistic is not just in the video sharing website market, it is in the search market in general, so YouTube ranks above Yahoo and MySpace as a general search engine!

This means that people are searching for video information more than ever before. There's no doubt in my mind that this is an opportunity for you to embrace the visual method of video to develop an even better relationship with your prospects.

Another way to develop rapport is using audio, whether that is live or recorded. Recorded audio is typically delivered as a podcast or as audio snippets to play on websites. Live audio is generally in the form of teleseminars or webinars.

A powerful and effective tool is to use both in conjunction to create the maximum impact. Remember, people can play almost any audio and video content whilst on the move on their mobile devices now, so you can be building a customer relationship with someone who is just on their way home from work on the train.

Pricing strategy with the customer in mind

Because of the whole shift of power to the customer online, your pricing strategy is going to be one of the key factors that could make or break your new online venture.

It's generally perceived by most people that costs are far lower with online retailers, after all online retailers don't need to have a shop front and it hardly costs a lot to run a website from a single computer server these days.

Clearly this begins to form the basis of your pricing strategy. If you are going to charge a lot more than offline providers, you'd better have a fantastic value offering.

Customers expect you to pass on those cost savings to them, so don't be greedy, pass some of these savings on. This is how Amazon grew so quickly because they sold books at a lower cost than offline retailers. They passed on the cost savings they made to the customer. It's really that simple, but I have seen many examples of people who ignore this fact and literally price themselves out of the market, whether too high or even too low.

eBay is another example of buying products cheaper than at retail stores. For the most part the only fixed cost an eBay seller has is warehousing their stock of goods.

Don't price yourself too high

You may think your service is worth a lot, however, the only perception that matters is that of the customer.

I often watch *Dragons Den* on TV and almost all of the time, the people bringing on the business offers value their own businesses too high.

We like to inflate our ego and make massive predictions about our success and I totally agree that we should dream and aim high; however we should also be realistic. If you have clear reasons for your high value, or a clear strategy to obtain that high valuation, then that's realistic.

A fun story which illustrates this is that of the epic fail of Fashion Cafe. It was a restaurant founded by a group of supermodels and fashionistas that served gargantuan sized burgers. It's kind of easy to see why it failed on that reason alone, but the biggest fail was charging $20 for a "Salad Extraordinaire", created exclusively for Naomi Campbell, which reportedly consisted of a glass of champagne, a pack of Newports cigarettes and two slices of tomato accompanied by an iceberg leaf. Famed restaurateur Tommaso Buti was the 'brains' behind the operation. He over-franchised the cafes, was accused of mismanagement and then followed Christy Turlington in selling his stake in the company.

A lot of the food was overpriced, and it didn't reflect the message which the supermodels were living by, after all you don't ever see them gorging away at mammoth-sized burgers and fries.

Don't price yourself too low either

Equally, pricing yourself too low and devaluing your products will get you nowhere fast. You might make some sales, but often you'll find that it's counterproductive because there's a limit you get to where people will start to think that there's a bad reason why your price is too low.

There's something more fundamental to consider if you are pricing yourself too low and that is the personal value that you are attaching to your solution, or yourself.

It's even more important to address this issue first because if you fundamentally believe that you are not worth the cost you place on your solution, then this negative mindset will underpin all your decisions and will cause you to make poor choices for your business in the future.

If you are under pricing because you want to undercut the competition, then I would say you are playing a very dangerous game. You are putting into force the law of diminishing returns whereby you'll have to sell even more just to make a profit. In most cases, people who use this strategy go into negative returns and that's when your business will start to suffer.

I find it interesting that new entrepreneurs have this habit of under pricing because they think that it will serve them best in the beginning. I say, consider what you think the price will be, and then double it to get the real market price. It's counter intuitive, but you will get just as many customers and earn a sensible return for your work.

Future customisation and personalization

The growth of choice online means that people are now requesting more and more personalization and customisation of products and services. It means that customers want to add their own tweaks and information and creative input into the solutions they are buying.

Sometimes it's choice of design, like when you go and buy a car you get to customise almost everything now, from the materials of the seats through to the colour of the dashboard.

I'm sure you've visited sites like Dell or HP computers where the level of customisation for personal computers and laptops is almost unparalleled. You can choose from customisations like processor speeds, hard disk sizes, graphics capabilities and even sometimes case design and aesthetic looks.

In a world where the customer is in control, your solution must offer personalisation.

Whatever niche you've decided to go into and depending on how you've defined what makes your business unique, now is the time to add what makes your solution personal.

By brainstorming this part of your business, you will also gain further clarity about what you are providing to your customer and how it helps to solve their problem better, with more personal care and attention.

Every individual is unique, so it stands to reason that every individual will want a slightly different solution to his problem.

If I went back to the hammer example, every single hand in the world is unique in size, strength and grip motion. Although it doesn't yet exist, if you could invent a hammer that has a variable grip to suit each individual's hand perfectly to deliver true maximum value from the hammering action, then you'd have a product that is unique, value driven, personalisable and probably award-winning too.

Building solutions with inbuilt customisable solutions

These are solutions that contain within them ways to change settings or customise to some degree the customer experience of that product or service, thereby giving the customer a certain degree of control over their experience of your product.

In computing it's easy to demonstrate this because most software has ways of configuring the appearance and functionality to suit the user.

In most cars there are controls to adjust seat height, width, angles and even temperature, giving the driver a custom seat suited to their body.

Office chairs are also good examples of products with built-in customisation. Most of the top end office chairs will have the ability to control height, lumber support and angle of the chair.

These are examples of solutions with inbuilt customisable options. Think about ways in which your solution can have these built into them such that when the customer is using your product or service online, they can somehow change it to suit their own needs.

Build solutions with Adaptable Customisable Solutions

These are solutions that have additional components that can be purchased separately to allow the customer to modify their original solution to meet their personalisation requirements.

This method often has a lot of benefits because it means additional sales of accessories or modules that are the very essence of long-term sustainable revenue for growth.

Going back to Apple as the example, you can buy so many different things to customise your iPod or iPhone now it's a market in itself. Besides buying covers and protective shields, there is now a range of third-party accessories to enhance the appeal of the original product and provide added value. Examples of these are speaker docks, alarm clock docks and integrated applications.

I really like the way online flower retailers offer this degree of personalization. Whenever you purchase flowers online, you'll often get ways to change the flower combination or add additional items to enhance the flower-giving experience. Whether that is extra champagne, chocolates or even a food hamper, there are always ways to customise. Of course, there is the option of adding a custom message.

When it comes to custom messages, there's no better example than Moonpig.com, a greetings card online retailer that allows the customers to completely design the card, contents, message and packaging. A total complete customisation based proposition.

Moonpig has really embraced that principle I mentioned about being the best at something and Moonpig are the best at greeting card customisation.

Ok, here's the part where you get to think about your product or service and how you can develop additional ideas to allow customer personalisation through external applications. Get this part right and you could make a lot of money because these kind of external solutions are typically low-cost production items with high margins.

The question you should ask is how are people likely to change my product or service to suit their needs and how might I be able to offer this change through another product or service.

Workshop 4: The value of your solution

As discussed, the value of your solution is very much determined by the perceived value by your prospects. These questions will help you to think more about the relationship of your solution to your customer.

1) What consistent problems or challenges are lots of people having that you know how to solve?

2) What makes your solution unique?

3) How does your solution relate to their problems with health, wealth or relationships?

4) Will your solution truly benefit your users (as opposed to only benefitting yourself)?

5) Will it enrich the user's experience and not mess up what already works for them?

6) Does your proposed solution already have consensus amongst potential customers?

7) How is your solution customisable?

8) How will you determine the price of your solution?

Notes

_____

_____

_____

_____

_____

_____

_____

_____

_____

SECRET 5

Build Solid Foundations

The captain and crew of the *Titanic* had the belief that nothing could sink the famous ship; however, when it came across the fatal iceberg that was to be its destroyer, nothing could have prepared it for the consequences of hitting the ice.

Petronas Towers, Kuala Lumpar, Malaysia

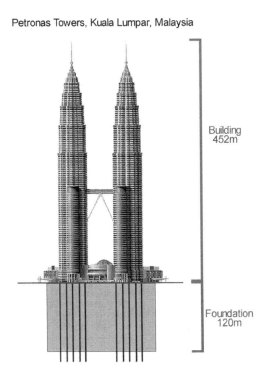

Building 452m

Foundation 120m

The people on board might have thought that they could get away with it, after all ice is just frozen water and the ship was far larger than the iceberg. However, an iceberg has over 80% of its volume underwater, and therein lies its strength and stability. No ship of any size was going to survive a collision with an iceberg.

It pays to have solid foundations. The tallest skyscrapers in any great city, all have foundations that go many metres deep and they are filled completely with concrete to solidify the base. The PETRONAS towers in Kuala Lumpar, Malaysia have foundations that are 120m deep.

These underlying principles are what keep most businesses profitable no matter what industry you look at. These are their business foundations and I believe that building these sets of skills will allow any business to grow strong in times of economic boom, but also weather the storm and hold steady in times of economic downturn.

Your business is not a hobby

There's kind of a double-edged sword when it comes to online businesses today; whereas on the one hand it is really cheap to get started in online business these days, the other comes back to bite the entrepreneur because the cheapness cultivates an attitude where they just don't care enough about their new online business to take it seriously.

I think it's partly because they haven't had to commit a large amount of capital to set up and so if they didn't succeed they wouldn't have lost very much money. For the most part you can get started for a small investment of £2000, which for a lot of people in this position is just one month's salary. If it failed, there's not a great loss there, perceptually.

You have to ask yourself this question, how serious are you about creating your own financial freedom through online business? Do you secretly fear failure so much that you don't even make the attempt, or only give it a half-hearted attempt so that in the event of failure you have some excuse?

Back in a time before the internet, when setting up a business meant having a large amount of starting capital, do you think if you set up a business then you would be so complacent? It certainly would matter if you failed because the amount of investment you were making would be perceived as substantial.

It's actually amazing in today's world of electronic communication and marketing, that so many people and I really do mean so many people, just seem to treat their new business venture like a hobby. Online business is not just for fun, it's not a place where you can just make a half-hearted attempt and you'll make money, it requires serious commitment of your time and energy.

You need to start right from the beginning, building a solid foundation, treating yourself and your business with the utmost respect.

The first thing you'll need to consider is your business infrastructure. This is everything needed to run your business, from the legal structure, expenses collection, through to making appointments and schedules. Even if you are working just for yourself at the beginning, making sure you have a good working infrastructure will allow you to grow quicker more effectively.

A space to create

Set up your working environment to suit the way you work. Make sure that you create a space which is clearly a workspace and organise your space accordingly. Keep it neat and tidy and ensure that everything you need is within that work zone.

Even if it is just a table in a shared space, get yourself a few folders and desk organisers and create a little setup that works for you.

It's just common sense I know, but you wouldn't believe how many people don't do this because they don't think it will make a difference. It absolutely makes a difference. How you do one thing is how you do everything, if you treat your working space and environment with respect and organisation, that attitude will translate into your business as well.

Tools to create

Having a good working environment is indeed the start, but after that you'll also need the right tools to get you started. There's nothing worse than starting a business with poor tools. Imagine giving a builder a set of rusty nails and half weathered wooden boards and asking him to build a fence. It certainly wouldn't be as good as one built with brand new wooden boards, strong rustproof nails and a strong hammer.

It's important to invest in the right tools, and for online business this means you'll need a computer that will last you a few years, and is capable of handling a lot of different tasks.

Think about it like this, in an organisation where many people perform different tasks, some more computer intensive than others, they have lots of different specifications for computer configurations, some more powerful than others. In your own little venture, you are going to be doing everything yourself: you are the CEO, the Chief of Everything Officer; you're the accountant, the director, the salesman and the janitor all at once.

Get yourself the right tools so you can do all these jobs with ease.

Besides a good quality computer the other most essential thing to have is a solid stable internet service provider and take a service that gives you high bandwidth. You're going to be spending a lot of time online, so it pays to have fast stable internet.

Whatever other tools you'll need for your business will depend on the type of business you are setting up, so do a little research. The main key to note is that with good tools you can create a good business; with great tools you can create a great business.

Workflow and systems

From an early stage in your new business, it's vital to develop a way of working which you can understand. This means that you need to have systems in place for the things you do and how the business operates.

When things work systematically in your business, you can be left to concentrate on developing the business and not worrying about how things get done.

It's a good idea to systemise things like invoicing, taking sales orders, creating reports for clients (if your business includes this) and various other administration tasks. Once you have a clear idea of how each part of your business will work, you can then concentrate on sales and generating revenue, knowing that when you get those orders and generate that business online, you'll have a systematic way of dealing with them.

It also means that when your business begins to grow, you'll have systems in place that will allow scalability more easily as you begin to outsource and build a team around you.

Ultimately your system is your IP, intellectual property, and one day you'll be able to sell your system because that is the most valuable thing you have in your business.

McDonalds is a great example of how a system is sold. The entire McDonalds franchise is a massive system of how things are done, from the management of staff to the way gherkins are placed inside

Big Macs. Every single operational task is systemised to the extent that a document can be produced about how it all works and more importantly, how someone else can replicate the system flawlessly.

The McDonalds franchise operations manual is many thousands of pages long spanning several volumes and it outlines their entire system of business. If you can document your system, you are well on your way to financial success.

Don't be afraid to invest your money where your mouth is

This comes back to belief because if you knew for sure that your investment would yield massive results and massive business success then you'd have no problem investing. However, for a lot of new businesses online, I've seen the owners making such small tiny investments into their business that it's no wonder they fail.

I know you can do things for free and I know that throughout this book I've talked about how you can for very little money, start to build an online business, however that doesn't mean that when there's a clear opportunity to invest into your business, that you should disregard it.

Your business is not a hobby, and even if it was I know some people who invest thousands of pounds into their hobbies, so doesn't your new online business deserve the same start?

When I was just starting out, in year 3 just before I began to make money, I made my first major investment into my business. For all those 3 years I had hardly spent anything substantial on the business itself or my own education. As I've said before, I literally did things the hardest way possible.

What I did was back in August 2004 I came across this conference all about online marketing to be held in Las Vegas. Having looked at the cost of attending and all the costs of the flights, the hotel and the cost of eating, it came to just over £2500 for the 5 days. I made the decision that if I was serious about my business and I was in it for the long haul, I knew that I had to make the investment in going.

Back then, £2500 was a lot of money and it still is a lot of money today to spend on a 5-day conference trip. I knew that the value I would get from meeting people and talking to experts in the industry would far exceed the money I paid to be there.

If you're serious about your business, invest in the opportunities that will present themselves to you and don't be afraid to do it.

Invest in training and education

In total hindsight, I can honestly say that if you want to rapidly accelerate your results, you should invest in training and education both on the mindset level and on the strategy level.

When I look back at how I approached my online business, I really did things the difficult way. I didn't take any training courses, I learnt almost entirely from online sources and I had to do a lot of trial and error to find out what worked and what didn't work.

I could have saved myself so much time and effort had I used a little more intelligence and found someone to teach me. I was unaware that there were any training courses and it didn't even occur to me to look for them.

If there's one thing I'd advise it's most certainly this point, invest in your knowledge and mindset. Since becoming successful I've had the opportunity to take many more courses and learn so many more things and having been on many trainings, I can honestly say that I wish I had done them in my first year of business.

There's nothing greater than learning from those who've been there before you; like the forefathers of great tribes, the elders always have greater insight from their experience and this kind of knowledge is absolutely invaluable.

Invest in help

Besides learning from great masters, it's also a good idea to invest in help. I never did think about things the right way from the start, but one thing I did do right was I realised that if I wanted to succeed, I would need to get other people to help me in every area of my life.

You should consider that you have an hourly rate of what you are worth, then whenever you are doing something that you feel you shouldn't be doing, ask yourself, could someone else be doing this for me at a rate that is lower than my own hourly rate? If the answer is yes, then you should consider it. I will be going into more depth on this point in a later chapter, as this is more relevant when you are growing your business after successfully starting up.

There are other areas where you can invest in help in the early stages of your start-up business. I would highly recommend that you hire a small company accountant. You could also hire a virtual PA to help with admin tasks. There are plenty of affordable services out there that can serve your needs quite well.

You must be prepared to devote your time to making it work

Talking about time, it's the one resource that we all have the same of, so on that note, we all have a level playing field. You can't tell me Richard Branson has more time than you do, so whenever someone tells me that they don't have the time, I will always state that they had the same time as anyone else.

It's not a matter of time; it's a matter of what you do with the time that makes the difference.

One of the things I learnt early on is that you will have to devote a lot of time and energy into your new business venture and you must be prepare to do it too. Remember this is an investment and if you don't feel that you can spare your time to get your new business idea started, then ask yourself what are you spending your time on instead and is that really more important than your financial freedom?

I've mentioned that I invested 3 years of my own life at the start of my journey into getting it working. That's 3 years with little to no revenue, whilst working every waking moment and choosing to spend my time building the business whilst my friends were out to play. I wanted financial freedom more than I wanted the short-term pleasure that my peers were pursuing.

To succeed, you must be prepared to make the time available by getting your priorities straight and working towards your highest values.

Understanding the business elephants in the room

There are three areas in a business that every entrepreneur knows they must get a handle on especially if you are weakest in those areas. You must first learn about them yourself, so that when you delegate them at a later stage in your business, you fully understand what is happening in those areas when your team members report to you.

If you've not heard of the term the 'Elephant in the room', it's an English idiom for an obvious truth that is being ignored or not being addressed. This is totally apt for these three areas because these are three areas which obviously need to be understood, but for the most part, new entrepreneurs tend to leave them unaddressed thinking that it's not important, especially internet entrepreneurs. In reality you are just putting off what you know needs to be done.

These are the areas of legal requirements, tax implications and financial reporting. Yes that's right, the three areas which I think all entrepreneurs will do their utmost to avoid, but avoid at your own peril, for they do come back to haunt you if you don't make sure you understand how they affect your new venture.

The Legal Elephant

- *(Elephas canonicus) The legal elephant is a rare species, often found grazing on fruit trees in the wild. They are indeed an incredible sight when you see them on the desert plains huddled in family groups for protection from the other beasts of the land. Their grouped nature lends well to protecting their young and often times you'll find them grooming their young ready, giving them haircuts and feeding them daily doses of Shakespeare.*

There are many things that you need to address at the beginning of starting a business and many of these will be the legal documentation that you need to complete in order to register your business for trading in your country. Every country has its own set of rules, but I bet that the same type of procedure will exist where you must tell some government agency that you intend to trade as a business.

This of course leads to many other items because you'll have to consider how your business should be set up legally. Are you a limited company, a sole proprietor or are you forming a partnership? You'll have to take all these items into consideration and decide what's best for you.

There are also other things which you must think about, for example if you are selling products online, you must define the terms and conditions of your sales and returns policy as well as the terms and conditions of doing business with you in general.

For any online business where you are collecting personal data, you must also define your privacy policy which must be clearly displayed on your website.

What's clear is that when you set this up properly, you won't have any repercussions later. I've heard of many stories where people get caught out and have suffered heavy fines for not having full registrations done. There was even one person I know who was fined over half a million dollars for what was deemed to be illegal trading because he didn't register with all the right legal channels.

The Tax Elephant

- *(Elephas miseratio) The tax elephant is an arrogant creature, often appearing at night to taunt and tease other sleeping wildlife with its eerily spooky night howl. In winter, it's often hard to spot the tax elephant because it tends to hibernate with great stores of beef jerky, emerging only to get mayonnaise once in a while.*

"Death, taxes and childbirth! There's never any convenient time for any of them," from *Gone with the Wind* by Margaret Mitchell.

It's true, we hate taxes, by golly we do, but we can't simply ignore them. Running a business means that you will have to yield some of what you earn to your government, for the privilege of doing business in their jurisdiction and living there.

This is most certainly an important area that you must understand. You have to find out what kind of tax implications you will have if you start trading business and that will determine so many other things for you including your pricing strategy later on.

If you are starting a business whilst you are in the employment of some other company, what does this mean for you from a tax perspective?

If you have no income at the moment and you are claiming state benefits, what does that mean from a tax point of view?

All these questions have to be asked and answered before you get underway. If you don't know where to begin on this one, try your local accountant or the Citizens Advice Bureau that should be able to point you in the right direction.

The Financial Elephant

- *(Elephas feneratus) The financial elephant is the most elusive of all the rare elephants. It's unusual shimmery yet translucent skin means that it can blend very easily into the background, much like a chameleon, however it has one thing that does give it away easily, and that is its often heavy grunting during mating season.*

It doesn't matter how much we all dislike doing the accounts, the fact of the matter is, business runs on money, and setting up a good infrastructure to organise and manage your money is going to be vital to success.

It's not difficult to create spreadsheets to monitor the incomings and outgoings of your new business. It's also very easy to create quick projection charts to see if you are on the right track.

Knowing your finances and your financial situation is just as important as the other two elephants. This means keeping excellent accounts and financial records of everything you spend and everything you make.

You need to learn about the financial cost of running a business, from the fixed and variable costs, to the cost of equipment and how to claim back depreciation on capital items of equipment etc.

There are a lot of things to record, but it will serve you well to maintain excellent records. It'll help you to make more accurate future projections, and when the time comes when you are seeking investment, you'll need to have accurate records to show tangible proof to potential investors, making the investment process easier, giving you a much higher chance of investment success.

Building your brand is building your business

People often confuse what a brand is, and in my mind a brand is in some way the fusing of your company's core values with your own. It is a message that you are conveying to the world, and this message is enforced by the way it is represented through imagery, sound and literature.

It's vitally important to recognise that your brand is not just your logo or your website design, it is far more than just that. In fact your logo adds very little to your brand at the beginning because you can have an incredibly compelling vision and message as your brand message and it can be represented with multiple brands. Such is the case with something like the Olympics. Though it has its five rings as the symbol of the Olympics, each time a new city is announced as the new hosts, a new logo is designed for that specific Olympic event. These become icons in themselves, which goes to show that it's the overall message that counts.

People buy Brands

Even though we'd hate to admit it to our friends, people buy brands. No matter what kind of industry or product you are talking about, people are making their purchase decisions based on the brand message.

It's also crucial to distinguish that buying brands is not just about buying the expensive brands; even your choice of supermarket is all about buying the brand and what it stands for, down to the individual food products within the supermarket. At whatever level people are buying at, depending on their purchasing power, there is still choice and people will choose according to what they perceive is the brand message.

In the UK supermarket industry, at the budget level there are companies like Aldi, Lidl and Somerfield, though the latter is bridging into the next level; even though you might believe that people are buying based on cost, they are ultimately, if even unconsciously, buying the brands.

To further illustrate this and encourage you to build a brand, here are some of the most recognised brands and what they originally stood for.

Volvo – safe cars
Apple – cool, simple-to-use technology
Zappos.com – delivering wow through customer service
Mercedes Benz – prestigious luxury cars
IBM – the most robust computer systems

Whenever I think about branding, I will always think of the example of Coca Cola and the story I've mentioned earlier in this book about the taste test and how in blind taste tests, Pepsi always wins, however, Coca Cola is the strongest global brand in the cola drinks market.

Online branding and how it helps

Having a web presence should be part of everyone's brand message. No matter what industry you are in, you need to have a web presence in order to first keep your options open for further development in the future. The interesting thing about having a website which is the digital component of your branding strategy is that a good website will almost certainly boost your brand, however, a poorly implemented website will damage your brand even more than not having a website all together.

It's interesting in today's business environment that people believe that they don't need a website. People are looking for websites now almost as certainly as they assume you should have a telephone contact number. The reason for this is because in most cases, it gives people a chance to research and do their due diligence on a company before potentially going into further interactions.

Think about this for a second, the last time you went to any social or networking function where you got handed a business card, when you got home and you thought about checking this person out, you visited their website first.

I know I do this all the time, so I'm sure other people must be doing the same thing. I do it because it allows me to get some background information before I proceed to further communication. This is a vital step in developing a successful business relationship with your customers and suppliers.

Your website is your second point of contact with your customers, so you must get this right from the beginning and have a solid foundation from which to work. Furthermore, in a research study conducted in 2009, it showed that a massive 76% of people will decide on further communication with you based on the quality and information on your website. So you can see that a bad website will surely damage your brand and drive prospects away.

Branding has been something I've been very strong on since the start of my business. Even in the early days when people were doing search optimisation on keywords, I was also spending some time on search optimisation for branding, only because I knew that it would serve me well in the long term.

I remember attending the very first conference in affiliate marketing and when I talked about my project, some people had already recognised the brand and commented on how professional and high quality both the brand and services were. In fact I remember someone asking me how many people worked with me on the project and when I stated that it was just me, they were shocked, thinking that there must have been a team of at least five people working on it. At this time I was hardly making any money from affiliate marketing, but I was building up for long-term success.

That's the kind of message and projection you want to be able to portray with what you are doing. If you can successfully convince people through your website that you are a big brand in their perception, and there is character and personality, then you know you've got a quality website.

Branding is the pill to long life

People over the ages are always seeking the magic formula or secret pill to long life and I think in the business world, the brand is the secret pill. This is the number one thing that is attributed to long-term growth and success when you get this right.

Once again to reiterate, your brand is a message. A message of your vision, your core values and how your company will show up in the world to solve the problem that you've set out to solve.

Have you ever heard of a 10-year-old company that didn't have a strong brand message? It doesn't exist, does it? Every company that has been around for a while survives because it has a strong brand.

When it comes to how the internet can help in this strategy to develop the long-term sustainability of your brand, there's a lot to consider. Just a short while ago, perhaps going back just 10 years, your online brand was solely represented by your website.

In recent years, the innovation of even faster communication methods has meant that your brand now extends beyond just your website. In fact it extends wide and far, many places of which are social media sites now which all help towards your overall message.

Having a long life as an internet brand is no longer just about providing a great product or service, it's about what your online branding represents.

This is good not only from a brand perspective, but from a search results point of view as well because Google has always favoured brands over non-brands. When it comes to its own search algorithm, Google is always finding ways to tweak it so that results will generally show visitors the more relevant results and these days the results have a slight tendency to show brand websites more than other websites.

Workshop 5: Getting Solid

Take a few moments to work through these questions that will get your mind thinking about your foundations:

1. How does your environment need to change in order to support your work and new venture?

2. Which area of knowledge or skills do you need to make the biggest investment in?

    a. Where can you find that training?

3. What are you prepared to stop doing in order to succeed?

4. What is your biggest elephant in the room?

5. What is the core message of your brand?

    a. Identify other brands in your market sector and ask yourself these questions about them:

        i. What core message am I getting from that brand?

        ii. Would I trust that brand and why?

        iii. Would I communicate with that brand and why?

For a video guide on setting up a new business visit **www.llm.im/freestuff**

Notes

_____

_____

_____

_____

_____

_____

_____

_____

_____

SECRET 6

Anything can be sold online

I've heard time and time again from many different people their belief that they don't have anything that could be sold online. When I hear that, I feel a challenge to find out what they are good at and to prove to them that there is something they can sell.

Just like the saying that 'everyone has a book in them', I believe that everyone has something they can sell online.

There is an abundance of good ideas

I think it's fair to say that everyone has a passion, even if it's watching TV, there's going to be a way to monetise that passion. It's just that you haven't found a mechanism or format to present your passion yet, so you don't think you could make money from it.

People make money selling the craziest things online, from dog training videos to candle wicks.

What is that thing you love doing, that you know you could show or teach someone else how to do it? I'm sure there is something you're great at, even if it's just one thing like making Cornish pasties, which has already been done by the way.

Everything starts with just one simple thing and then it expands. Whoever thought something as simple as a doughnut could become a global business in the brands of Krispy Kremes and Dunkin Doughnuts?

If you've come up with a solution to a problem, then the question you need to ask is whether people would be willing to pay for the solution; if you think not, then ask yourself, what else could you add to the solution to make it more valuable so that people would pay for it?

There are multiple ways to view a problem so the question isn't about the solution, it's about how the solution is presented. Take for example lettuce. Market research shows that there is a percentage of people who lack time to prepare food and instead of buying a whole lettuce and chopping it, they'd prefer to buy ready chopped and now even ready washed lettuce.

Imagine if that chopped lettuce was sold to you in a bunch that you just grabbed and threw into a bag, which you had to weigh to get the price. That's not as appealing as the clear plastic wrapping with all the details printed and ready to go. The way it is presented now in supermarket shelves makes it higher value. That's all down to presentation, after all, the lettuce is the same.

In fact, the very act of presenting the lettuce well gives it even more value. The same quantity of chopped lettuce would be half the price if purchase whole.

Say your passion was in kites and flying kites, you might consider becoming a kite retailer, kite flying teacher or perhaps you could specialise in custom kite designs. There are many different angles to approach an industry. One great way to determine what people want is to visit forums of that topic and run polls and surveys to find out what their needs are. You'll get lots of great feedback and probably clearer ideas on how you could monetise your passion.

Using publications

There are lots of fantastic publications that you can pick up and read which will give you plenty of ideas. In fact, you could go into a newsagent and find a magazine on just about any topic these days. Incidentally, if a magazine exists for your chosen industry, then it's a good sign that there is a market for those services.

A few good magazines to get fresh ideas from are *The New Scientist*, *The Economist* and also *Engadget* magazine. You can find out about the latest scientific discoveries and capitalise on them, or you could read about the changes in the economy and capitalise on those. Alternatively, reading *Engadget* will tell you all about the latest technology and perhaps you'll find an opportunity in there.

You're probably thinking it isn't that easy. Well I'm here to tell you it really is, though you have to practice and train your mind to see opportunities because for the most part people aren't brought up to look for opportunity.

Just to show how it's done and what's actually possible, I've got in front of me the magazine, *NewMediaAge*, 17th February 2011 publication.

Page 3, there's an article called 'Tesco set to launch separate online shop for F&F range', Tesco are about to create an online shop just to sell their F&F clothing range. You could create a site which writes about their F&F clothing range and test it against other products of the same price and category and see how they fare. It would be a review and test site. You would then join up to the F&F affiliate program and pass on customers who read your reviews. You can also become an affiliate of other similar price range retail clothing stores and direct visitors to those sites. All the time you'll make commission on any visitor who ends up buying at any one of these online stores. That's a simple yet effective idea because focusing on just reviewing and testing the Tesco brand clothing is an easy set of keywords to optimise a site for.

Page 4, 'Salaries for digital roles up 8% as clients recruit for in-house teams'. This one is easy, you could create an online recruitment website which focuses entirely on how to recruit and identify better candidates for social media and digital roles. That's unique enough that people would come along and know you for just knowing what makes a good social media hire.

Page 28, 'Fair of Face', I jumped ahead as there are too many ideas already to consider. This is an article about how having a presence on Facebook is a must for any consumer-facing brand, but just being there isn't enough, you need to be truly engaging. There's an opportunity to set up a service that just concentrates on how to transpose your brand onto Facebook and make your page engaging. Remember, you don't have to do the technical work, you can pay someone else to do it!

I think by now you should have a good grasp that ideas are literally everywhere. Opportunities are in abundance and all you have to do is to go to the magazine store and buy a few magazines.

Using guru forums

Guru or expert forums are a fantastic way to get new ideas. Typically at these places you have a lot of experts discussing the industry they are in and normally you can get a lot of information out of those conversations.

Since humans like to complain, that's what forums are for, a place to voice a problem. Have you ever heard of a forum where people get together just to say how great everything is and how wonderful life is for them? No, and I don't imagine you ever would because that's not in our nature.

Where there is complaint, there is a problem. Where there are problems, there are opportunities to find solutions for those problems. Try places like affiliate forums and internet marketing forums, these places have a lot of great ideas about new marketing strategies for online and also many of them will discuss new markets coming online and how to monetise those new markets.

Any information can be packaged and sold

People find it hard to study long term and assimilate information, just like going to university; however people do find it easy to consume packets of information that are quick and easy to access, like books.

I have a friend who is currently doing a tree surgery course. I asked him, isn't it easy, surely all you have to do is get a ladder, climb up and cut the tree down. He told me that the course was 2 years long and that there were students there who had come from overseas to take this course.

You could package that information into a smaller condensed format and deliver it online, charge a smaller fee than the course and give overseas people greater access to that knowledge. You've just created a new business.

You see, as I've mentioned, people buy packaging. If you can present information in a digestible format, people will be more than happy to pay for it. Typically this has been in the form of books, but these days online you have many options including eBooks, video, audio, membership sites and many other ways.

The best way to package this information is into small digestible chunks, but not too small otherwise the consumer will find it hard to get their teeth sunk into it. Presenting the package is just as important. Even if you are delivering a video online, you can create the illusion that it's a package by generating a DVD box image and putting cover art onto it.

The take away point here is that your core business is your intellectual property (IP). At the end of the day, all the successful brands and businesses out there including offline and online, are all selling IP. McDonalds is selling a system, their IP. Apple is selling their IP because an iPad on its own is just a piece of metal, glass and plastic; however when you add Apple's software and applications to it, it becomes a whole lot more useful.

Even coffee is IP. You might think Starbucks is selling you coffee, but actually they are selling you the perception of high quality coffee at low prices, farmed fairly and roasted in a particular way which creates their taste. There is a complete system in place to deliver that promise, and that's what you are buying. If any part of that system fails and you end up either with bad tasting coffee or overpriced coffee, you wouldn't buy it, and they would lose your custom.

Intellectual property is the number one product you have in your stables that will be the life blood of your business. It's the one thing that will ensure your company has future value.

People are prepared to pay well for the right perceived solution. What I mean with this is that sometimes your solution may not be perceived as correct by the buyer. If you can determine why, you can change your solution to meet the perception of the buyer and then you'll be able to charge double the price and the buyer will still pay you for the solution.

There is always a market

No matter how small, there is always a market and now with online communications providing every user with a global reach, the market just has greater access to your services.

In a global market, there is always someone looking for your answer.

I did a random search on Facebook and came across a few groups around phillumeny. In case you don't know what this is (I certainly didn't), it's the hobby of collecting match related stuff, like matchboxes.

There were a grand total of just over 270 people on these groups, but on a wider Google search I could see a whole selection of websites around the topic and I would imagine that there's a market for these people. What you would sell to them I don't know, however it exists and it's only a matter of creativity to find out what needs these people might have.

Sometimes you don't even know where that market might exist; however something you do just resonates with a certain group and all of a sudden you are serving a solution for which some people are prepared to pay for.

I have a site that is targeting the USA as a geographical market, however for some reason, as well as US visitors, we also have a strange skew of Romanian visitors and this is something we didn't plan for. For whatever reasons, the Romanians find the site appealing; perhaps it's the colour scheme, perhaps it's the layout or logo. It's too hard to tell, the web is so organic that sometimes you've just got to let it be.

Niches are no longer confined to geo locality

There is always a market online, no matter how niche your idea or product is. The internet has made it possible to serve and deliver globally, which means that we are no longer confined by our location when it comes to online business.

There are suppliers in Hong Kong who specialise in mobile phone cases. They sell these across the planet at very affordable costs. There are t-shirt designers and makers in Thailand who sell globally as well. Anyone, anywhere can start to create something and you've instantly got a potential global market to sell to.

One of my clients sells extremely niche tooling machines which clamp wires to a certain ISO standard required for high safety applications, for example in car electronics. They are based in the UK in Kent, however their biggest growth market now is China and the internet has allowed them to reach that market, open up communications and create a brand new revenue stream that just 5 years ago might have seemed too difficult to attempt.

Defining your niche, USP and target market is vital to success

A USP is a unique selling proposition and I'm sure that you've heard this term before, as most people have in business. It's what makes your product or service more unique than your competitors. The businesses that succeed are generally those who come to market with something that makes them different.

If it's something that others can replicate, then make sure you take it to levels beyond their reach. For example, Zappos.com came along and made excellent customer service their unique proposition, but many companies could also report that their customer service is excellent, too. What Zappos.com did was take customer service to another level that other businesses simply couldn't emulate. They went so far beyond what was considered good customer service that they literally redefined what excellent customer service meant.

Identifying your niche is also an extremely important task. Typically in any given market, it's possible to identify an even tighter segment within that market and create for yourself a much more alluring opportunity. Niches are driven by ultimate desire or extreme pain. The more your prospects feel these opposing emotions about a problem, the more likely you'll be able to monetise that specific niche.

The workshop at the end of this chapter will help you to get further clarity on your niche.

Identifying your target market though personification

Also, top of the list of things to do is to clearly identify who your potential customers are. It's no longer ok just to define them by their general demographics like age, gender, income and interests. In today's competitive economy, you need to be able to get into the psyche of your target customer in order to understand their needs and sell them the solution they need.

One of the key mistakes a lot of entrepreneurs make when starting out, is assuming that the customer is just like them. This couldn't be further from the actual truth. To get clarity, I developed a method called "Ideal Target Personification (ITP)" to define the target customer.

The way I like to do it, is to focus in specifically on a single person and even give them a name. In this process, you will get so deep into the target's mind that you will begin to see the nuances that give you an opportunity to make your solution better than the competition.

The way it works is you begin with the standard demographic information to give you a platform to explore your thinking. Consider all those factors you generally would like age, location, race, income levels, relationship status etc.

Once you've finished identifying the target market on this broad level, which is where most people stop, we are going to take this deeper. At this point we focus all our attention on a single individual who is perceived to be the perfect customer for your solution.

Give this person a name and figure out what year this person would have been born in. Remember this is the perfect customer. Now that you have an idea of whom this person is, it's time to take this all the way back to when this person was born. This is where we will begin to write the autobiography of this person from their birth, all the way to the present day.

This is an in-depth process where you must write everything you can imagine about the person. Here are some questions you should ask:

- What was their childhood school like?

- Did this person have many friends growing up?

- Where did they go to university, if at all, and if not, why not and what did they do instead?

- Are they interested in sports, or politics or languages?

- Where did they meet their life partner?

- What kind of vacations would they take? Did they prefer ship cruises or adventure hikes?

The list is endless, the more depth and detail you can manage, the more insight you will develop. You should end up with an autobiography at least five pages of A4 long. Now you have the most incredible document in your hand because within this document you are going to see the reasons why this person needs your solution. You'll also discover that many of the things you've written about this person can become messages in your marketing campaigns. It'll give you insight into how you will phrase your company literature and advertising.

Some people ask me whether this is being too specific; wouldn't you be isolating potential customer groups when you get so detailed about one person? My answer to that is, no. You would not be ignoring the rest of the target market.

You see, every customer aspires to be the perfect customer. I believe that by profiling just the perfect customer, you are in fact encapsulating the entire potential market.

Why is every customer aspiring to be the perfect customer?

Let's take some examples. The ideal customer for a TV set is one that buys the most expensive one, asks for an installation service and purchases a 10-year extended warranty. We all aspire to be this customer, after all, do we want to install it ourselves, or suffer the risk of no warranty after 6 months? The only reason we don't buy the full package is because we have a problem, we don't have the money, but we aspire to have the money.

Take another example, the perfect customer for an accountant is the new client who asks the accountant to do everything for them, and refers additional customers. We all want the best possible, so it's clear that by identifying the absolute profile of the perfect customer, we can see what all customers are aspiring to.

What about the perfect client for a landscape gardener? That would be someone who needs a complete garden transformation, without holding back due to finances, but just going all the way with no expense spared. Would we all love that for our gardens, too?

Same can be said for any product or service, we all aspire to be the perfect customer, it is our own resource limitations that prevent us from being that perfect customer.

Business personification to facilitate the conversation

In the same way I've described how to personify a target individual, you should also create a profile and personify your business.

In a similar way, but not using demographics, you must choose how your company would be represented by a character, then write a full biography of your character that represents your business.

This will provide you with a deep insight into who your business is, and how it could be seen by your potential customers. Using this persona, imagine them having a conversation with your target customer.

Imagine the words they would be using and how they would behave with each other. Is it corporate professional, perhaps it's fun and cheeky? However the interaction occurs, write it all down and this begins to form the basis of yet more of your company information.

It gives you an idea of how to present yourself and your brand and also gives character to your brand as well.

Selling other people's services or products

In a world where people are always looking for new ideas or trying to invent something unique, it might serve to remind you that some of the largest businesses in the world are businesses that simply sell other people's products.

Selling other people's products is an easy way to get started because you don't have to make anything, and if you are selling other people's services, you don't even have to deliver anything.

You get a lot of help straight up front because if the product already has some market reputation, your job selling it becomes a whole lot easier. You also save on marketing costs because you'll have the parent company marketing as well as you.

The best example of this model is the supermarket. This is one of the oldest trades, originally bringing people together into one location to enable the customers to get access to multiple products and services all at once.

Moving into this century, the supermarket is essentially the biggest retailer of other people's products. Shelves are stocked full of different and competing brands, yet the supermarket company is making a huge profit for providing the services of delivering those products to the consumer.

In much the same way, a mortgage broker provides customers with a range of suitable mortgages to secure a property. They are selling the services of many banks and building societies to customers in this way because customers like to compare the market, and often times, they do not have the skill or expertise to identify what makes a better deal, so a broker is introduced, like an advisor.

In the same way that you can sell other people's products or services in the real world, you can also do the same online. eBay is a perfect example which is a site helping other people to sell their products, but they themselves are not selling anything other than an easy-to-use auction and shopping system.

The affiliate programme

The affiliate programme is a unique marketing model that was introduced very early on back in 1989 and its origins are based on traditional multi-level marketing models. I'm sure that once or twice you might have heard of the original network marketing programmes like Avon or Nutrilite, or more famously Amway, because of their high profile recruitment strategy that often put people off and gave network marketing a bad name.

The affiliate programme model online continued to have a quiet existence but it did gain some supporters within early adopting industries such as cyber-erotica and in 1994 CDNOW launched a programme to allow music review sites to link through and earn a commission on music sales.

However, it wasn't until 1996 when Amazon adopted and remodelled the affiliate programme model and made it even more accessible, that it really became a viable marketing option for other industries.

Affiliate marketing is the marketing practice which compensates the marketer or "affiliates" for bringing in customers based on the affiliate's own work. The beauty of this is that affiliates only get paid when a visitor becomes a customer; so effectively as a company, you could have an entire online marketing team without having to pay them until they produce results.

Commissions could be based on a fixed bounty per sale, or on percentage of sales. With affiliate programmes becoming more advanced, there are also many different hybrid variations of commission structures that give added flexibility to both the affiliate and parent company.

The Opportunity

It was September 2001 when I was sitting down at my little computer desk in my bedroom and I was looking around the Internet searching for ideas that might inspire me into action. You see at this time of my life, I had been out of work voluntarily for 7 months after quitting my job because I had come to the realisation that it wasn't what I wanted to do.

I had only spent 3 years in that software company that delivered trading systems to tier one banks globally. It was something that I always thought I wanted to do since I decided on taking computer sciences for my university degree. I always imagined that I'd make a killing as an IT specialist in the finance world, and I did.

However, despite having some savings, my prolonged time off period in the summer of 2001 had taken its toll and I found myself in debt to the tune of around £20,000, a position that I had never thought I'd be in.

It was that moment in time in the autumn of 2001 that I came across an article on Yahoo news that was discussing the rise of affiliate marketing in the online gambling sector. It was one of those unusual situations where I had no interest in marketing, gambling or even news at the time, yet this article piqued my interest and I continued to read on.

It turned out that the article was talking about the affiliate marketing model and how it would impact on this fledging industry at the time. It predicted that affiliate marketing would be responsible for billions of dollars of revenue generated and all in the space of 5 years. I knew instantly there was an opportunity there.

I began researching the model, how it was applied and what I could do to get a piece of the action; before I even knew it, I had started work on my very first project, which to this day is still running and turning over passive income.

The news article on Yahoo was wrong, it turned out that affiliate marketing had a much wider-reaching effect, touching all industries, and now you can find affiliate programmes attached to almost every online website that sells some products or services.

How can this work for you?

Well, if you are interested in something and you have a passion for it; if you don't have any products or services in that category, you can go and find other people's "stuff" online and find out if they have an affiliate programme for you to join. Most reputable online brands and websites are more than likely now to have an affiliate programme.

All you have to do is think about how you would market that company's solution online. Whether you do it by creating a website, or by creating a huge social network, the choice is yours. At this stage, you'll need to exercise the creativity that I talked about earlier. You have to be super creative to think up incredible ways of using various internet technologies to create marketing strategies that you can implement and promote other people's products.

As far as I can tell, there are four main legitimate ways that I've seen affiliates make the most of affiliate programmes. I say legitimate because the commissions in certain affiliate industries can be so great that illegal spammers and rogue operators also use more guerrilla and black marketing tactics. These are to be avoided at all costs; short-term gains here can often lead to long-term pains everywhere else.

Comparison site

The comparison site model is one where the site lists the services or products of various suppliers and provides their own criteria on which one is better and for what reasons.

Typically customers will go to comparison sites to get a better deal or to look for cheaper alternatives to the solution they've discovered themselves.

These kinds of sites are relatively easy to run, though often they will require more substantial technical knowledge to operate because it involves data comparisons to create the analysis reports to show site visitors.

Some examples of these include CompareTheMarket.com or MoneySupermarket.com that are both insurance and financial product comparison search engines. Both are highly complex and are now multimillion pound companies themselves, probably negotiating separate deals with the financial product providers on a more private partnership arrangement. However, I suspect they started out as small sites running off the affiliate programmes to get started.

Other examples of comparison sites that sell other people's products include Kelkoo, Pricerunner and NextTag. These sites will present you the products and a range of suppliers where you can purchase them. When you click on their links, they will redirect you to the seller's website and that's how they earn their commission.

To make a comparison site successful, you need to have lots of data points to input about all the services or products you are comparing, so it really only works if the companies you deal with have sophisticated back end data exporting processes and you have sophisticated data importing tools.

The investment to get this type of site up and running is extremely high; however, the rewards can be extremely high too.

Blogger

This is probably the quickest and easiest way to get started with affiliate programmes and that is to host a blog about something you are deeply passionate or interested about. The best bloggers in the world in their categories are often seen as gurus and will attract a lot of organic search engine traffic.

It's easy to set up a site like this and start to blog. There are plenty of systems which can run a blog, all of which will be covered in chapter 8. Once it is up and running, all you have to do is to find either products or services around the topic of your discussion, and place them strategically on your website to attract other interested visitors to click through on them and earn you revenue.

Affiliate programmes will always have a back end system that allows you to log in and view your statistics and obtain marketing materials. Typically, these would be tools like advertising banners, email sales copy and possibly RSS data feeds, depending on the sophistication level of the programme.

As an example of how influential a blogger can become, one of our gambling websites has a blog that discusses a lot of what's happening in the world of celebrity and Las Vegas. As a result of our blog posts and internet reach, in 2010 I was invited to the Las Vegas red carpet premiere of *The Expendables* movie and was given a complete 4-day super-VIP treatment with photos and interviews with the movie's cast members, as well.

You see, if you can provide an influential voice, you can be noticed online and that can translate to serious offline goodies!

If you ever wanted to know how much you could make as a blogger, look no further than the blogs of Michael Arrington (Techcrunch) and Om Malik (GigaOm). Both run highly successful technology blogs that are read by thousands of subscribers. These two A-List high profile tech bloggers are turning hobbies into businesses that make over $2 million a year.

Technorati, a blog search engine, ranks Techcrunch as the fourth-most-linked-to blog on the internet. GigaOm ranks 34, a still impressive number given that Technorati tracks more than 86 million blogs.

A little closer to home here in the UK and outside the technology sector, Susanna Lau started a fashion blog title Stylebubble back in March 2006. Lau is currently considered to be Britain's biggest style blogger and her online diary now gets 300,000 unique users a month. She graduated from University College London and started working in digital marketing, where she met her boyfriend, fellow blogger Steve Salter, and started her blog purely as a creative outlet. As its reputation grew, so did Lau's: she was headhunted for the fashion magazine *Dazed and Confused* to be their new online commissioning editor.

With her audience figures Lau is one of the few bloggers who could drive some serious revenue from her blog. A site as strong as Stylebubble's, which has about 600,000 page impressions (the number of times a page is clicked on) per month, can expect to sell ads at £12-15 per thousand page impressions. Lau has commented that she didn't really want to make blogging her living, so she doesn't really take advertisements on the site.

As you can see, blogging can be a great model if it works for your topic.

Review site

The review site is my personal favourite because I feel it provides the visitors with truly valuable information about a service or product that they wouldn't get anywhere else.

The review site is one step further than the blog site, in that a review site will generally explore the product or service to its entirety, to provide an in-depth analysis of the product or service and an objective review.

Visitors love these types of sites because they contain valuable information to allow the visitor to make a better buying decision. Oftentimes online buyers will seek the opinion of several review sites before they make up their mind.

As a review site, you must be totally objective and provide real advice to your discerning buyers. Review sites will often review both bad and good products on the market and will openly discuss the benefits and flaws of the product.

A good example of a successful review site is Dpreview.com. This site reviews all digital photography products from compact cameras and SLR cameras to lenses and other accessories as well. The site is focussed around the in-depth reviews, but it also has provision for a blog, a forum for discussion and also a members' gallery.

Social networker

Very new to the scene is the social networker method of promoting affiliate products. This is new because at the time of writing, social media is still quite new to the internet. With this method, you don't even need a website to get started.

This requires that you have a certain perspective on a topic, much like the blogger; however instead of having a single website blog to voice your opinion you do it on social media platforms like Facebook, Twitter, Orkut or any other social networking platform.

The idea is to build up a veritable list of followers and listeners whose trust you will gain by providing great insight and knowledge. Periodically you can market a new product to them by email or social media discussion.

I would say that this method requires a different type of hard work. The work involved revolves mostly around gaining trust and becoming an expert in your topic, whilst at the same time employing methods to attract people to your social networking landing page.

Using an affiliate programme as a producer

If you are a producer of a product or service, you can use an affiliate programme to effectively create a marketing team for a small budget, and pay them only on successful sales.

I won't spend long on this section because at this stage it isn't important to setting up a new online business. Having an affiliate programme has massive advantages as you can see from all the above examples. It's a strategy that is better employed once your company is established with products and you're looking to expand and grow your company to the next level. More of this will be discussed in my next book about how to grow your online business to the next level and beyond.

Doing joint ventures and partnerships

There are certain circumstances when doing a joint venture (JV) is a more viable route to take with a particular company. JVs are typically done when the relationship with the partner company is extremely strong. This might be an existing business relationship or a relationship obtained through other means, but it doesn't matter how it is achieved; what's important to distinguish here is that this kind of relationship is more intricate than the affiliate programme arrangement.

In a JV deal, there are many more variables taking place, with possibilities of exclusivity and higher returns for both parties. When a JV takes place, the two parties typically work much closer together on all activities because both parties are vested in the selling process and are jointly responsible for its success or failure.

Getting a joint venture with a company is quite difficult if this is the first online business you are embarking on. That's not to say it's impossible, however most companies will only joint venture with people who already have a track record and proven results.

One of the reasons why it can be so lucrative is because you could become the only supplier of a product to an online market, though typically a company will JV with a few select people to reduce risk.

One great method of spotting this type of potential is to look out for suppliers of products to a certain geographic market, where they currently have little to no online mechanism to market or deliver their product. You can step in to prove that you know exactly how to bring their product to the online market and create the JV proposition that way.

A partnership can come in any form and a good real world example is the story of Reggae Reggae Sauce and its founder Levi Roots. Knowing that he needed an investment partner to bring his sauce to the market, he went onto the popular entrepreneurs programme *Dragons Den* and managed to strike a partnership with Peter Jones and Richard Farleigh.

This proved to be a crucial move because the investment he made opened up an incredible partnership that has to this date been one of the most successful ventures to appear on the programme. As well as being sold in most major supermarkets, the brand is also partnered with top food brands such as Slug and Lettuce, JD Weatherspoon and Subway. Levi is estimated to have a net worth of about £8million now.

Joint ventures can happen with any size of business as long as it serves the goals of both parties involved. In the online world, one of the largest joint ventures to happen was between Baidu, China's largest search engine, and Rakuten, Japan's largest e-commerce website. In the deal, both companies agreed to jointly invest $50 million over three years in a venture to build a B2B2C (business to business to consumer) online shopping mall for Chinese-internet users.

Becoming a champion

Another way to capitalize on other people's ideas is to help them to sell their idea online, effectively becoming a champion of their cause. If you have the skill and expertise to run online marketing solutions, and you don't have any ideas yourself, you can become a solution provider and market yourself as a service to those who want to spread their idea.

Essentially you become a freelance agent working for yourself but helping other people to get their projects off the ground. You could become an exclusive writer for a newspaper or a charity. If your core skill is in communication and you have excellent success in promoting ideas through language, then perhaps this is the route for you.

An alternative way in which you can capitalize on big ideas is to become a supporter of someone else's idea and ride the momentum that idea already has, developing a new site around the same topic.

For example right now, Jamie Oliver has a big cause that he is spreading, and that is the fight against obesity and educating people about how good cooking can make a difference. You could easily piggy back off this cause and idea and produce a website which talks all about healthy living, healthy eating and cooking healthy great-tasting food.

There's no reason why you couldn't help the movement by adding your voice in conjunction, and together doing good as well for society.

So have you got something you want to sell?

Whether it is an idea, a service or a product, you are still selling a solution to a product; any solution can be sold online because the internet is one big solution-providing machine. I said before that search engines are the ultimate solution finder because anyone going online is looking for something.

They are in seeking mode, and they are seeking a solution to a problem. The problem might be that they want to visit the theatre that night and can't find tickets, or the problem might be that they don't want to risk their car breaking down and leaving them stranded.

Whatever the problem, they'll look for a solution online; if they find a solution that looks good, feels trustworthy, seems to understand their problem and provides real value, then they will be more than happy to pay for it online.

Workshop 6: Niche and Target Personification

Have you thought about what you want to sell online now? Perhaps it's the service or product you've been thinking about throughout reading this book, or maybe you were just looking for an idea in this book.

If you are unsure about your idea at this stage, try our guide about ideas: **www.llm.im/freestuff**

In workshop 4 we worked on your solution and what you are bringing to the table. I'd like to help you to create a more powerful solution because the best way to 'corner a market' is to create the market. This exercise will challenge you to look deeper into your market to identify what your customers' needs and motivations are.

Let's niche

1) Viability test – need yes answers to all four in order to proceed to Positioning.

    a. Are your prospects experiencing extreme pain, or irrational passion?

    b. Are your prospects looking for solutions proactively?

    c. Are there little to no perceived solutions in the market place?

    d. Is there at least 1 in 1000 people looking for a solution right now?

2) Positioning

    a. In what area does your prospect have an emotional,

irrational need driven by a strong fear or desire?

b. What is the unmet need that you can solve with your solution?

c. How can you present your solution in a way that solves their needs? (Is the solution a product or service, and how would it be presented?)

d. Where is the prospect searching for solutions, can you find them?

Ideal Target Personification (ITP) exercise

In this exercise, I want you to go and find out as much demographic information about your ideal market segment as possible. Then identify a single person within which it can embody the ideal customer, then give them a name and write their entire life history. I really do mean their entire life history. This should be about 3-4 pages long.

- Start with the year they were born, and work towards now. E.g., John, who is now 35, was born in 1974. His parents were from.... His hometown was.... When he was 6 he went to St Klingon School, at 17 he studied physics, history and politics. Etc.

- Some example details to consider:

  o What was their childhood school like?

  o Did this person have many friends growing up?

  o Where did they go to university, if at all, and if not, why not and what did they do instead?

  o Are they interested in sports, or politics or languages, and what are the reasons why they have their interests?

  o Where did they meet their life partner?

  o What kind of vacations would they take? Did they prefer ship cruises or adventure hikes?

- o Do they have children? Do they want children? If so, how many and why?

- o What is their living space like? Why did they pick the furniture they have?

These are all ideas; you should write what makes sense for your target.

For a more detailed discussion on questions to consider with the ITP exercise, visit **www.llm.im/freestuff**

Notes

_____

_____

_____

_____

_____

_____

_____

_____

_____

SECRET 7

You own biggest library in the universe

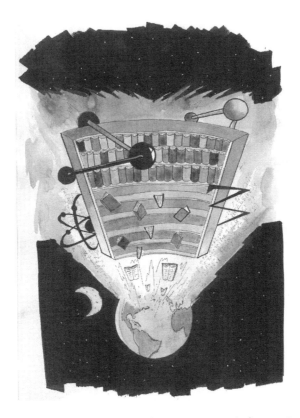

We are at a stage in time when there is more information available to us online than ever before. In fact, if you collected all the written information of all time up to now, you still wouldn't come close to the information that is available at your fingertips.

The internet is truly the biggest library in the universe and it's now accessible by everyone. This chapter is going to cover how to deal with so much information and how to make the best use of the internet, from the perspective of information.

The trouble about having so much information is that you have to develop strategies to read only what is necessary. It's true that you can pretty much learn everything you need to about doing business online via the internet. The only challenge becomes how to find the best information and how do you know it is the best?

This is the main difference between learning from trusted sources in training environments, to searching for it yourself online. Either method of learning will get you to the end results; each one will differ in speed and implementation depending on your own learning strategy.

I just want to prepare you for the next couple of chapters as it's about to get a tiny bit jargonistic and technical, but only a tiny bit. The thing is, you're reading a book about online business, so no matter how technophobic you are, there are things you need to know and things you need to learn. Remember that if technology is your elephant in the room, then it's time to acknowledge it and start to train that elephant to become useful and effective.

Information universe

There's more information available to us than in all of history. Isn't that an incredible thing to be a part of? Right now, most of the developed world has portable devices that will allow them to access this information source, at any point in time, anywhere on the planet.

If knowledge is power, then every individual is now more powerful than ever. However, like I've said before, it's all about the action, so knowledge is not enough, you have to apply the knowledge into action.

Google is the number one place to start looking for information. Just to give you some idea of the size of Google, Google runs over one million servers in data centres around the world, and processes over one billion search requests and about 24 petabytes of user-generated data every day.

Let's get some perspective on what a petabyte is. We are all familiar with a megabyte (mb) and a gigabyte (gb) by now. A DVD is typically 6gb of information. A 12 megapixel camera will take high quality photos at around 5mb per image.

A petabyte is 1000 terabytes. A terabyte is 1000 gigabytes, so a petabyte is 1,000,000 gigabytes. This means Google processes over 24,000,000 gigabytes per day, that's the equivalent of 4.8 million DVDs per day. That's a lot of information.

YouTube is also now the second largest search engine in the world. This means that more people are searching for video content than ever before. The rise of YouTube has created many success stories in itself which goes to show that you don't need a website to make money online.

I love the story of Michelle Phan and how she came about her success by creating videos on YouTube. It was reported that Phan wanted to work in the fashion and beauty industry in the niche of make-up, but having applied for jobs in the top make up companies, she didn't get the opportunity to do so. She decided to make the videos herself and post them on YouTube.

Since joining in 2006, she has created over 130 videos that have been viewed over 290 million times in total. Her channel has been viewed over 50 million times. Her videos have a signature style where she incorporates her voice-over instruction with music and text subtitles. Her videos are created entirely using iMovie on a MacBook Pro. As a result of this success, she is now a spokeswoman for Lancôme and it has been reported that the deal, which included channel sponsorship, came in at seven figures. Not bad for creating a few videos on a laptop and uploading them!

Wikipedia is another interesting phenomenon that shows the sheer scope of information and more accurately user-generated information. For those who haven't yet encountered it, it's like an online encyclopaedia of knowledge about anything that's worth knowing about.

What's interesting about Wikipedia is that the content is completely user generated. It currently has over 3.5 million articles, which is seven times greater than the size of the *Encyclopaedia Britannica*, historically known as the most scholarly of encyclopaedias, with articles written by about 100 full time writers and about 4000 contributors.

Filter the noise

Just as the universe has background cosmic noise, so does the internet. So with so much information available, one of the key skills to learn right now is how to filter out the information so that you are getting only what you need, you don't overload yourself with too much, or get too distracted by all this information.

There are many ways to help you to maximise the information and make full use without suffering the side effects of time wastage.

The best and most recommended way is to have someone do the research for you! I know it sounds like a cheat, however if you are researching the best way to do something online, perhaps you are looking for how to create a Wordpress blog, there are hundreds of articles on the topic, so how do you know which one to read? Do you read all of them? Do you read ten of them and choose one that you think might work, only to find it doesn't? That's a lot of potential time-wasting activities. Why not find someone to do the initial research for you?

You can hire an intern or a cheap outsourcer to do this for you and all you have to do is provide clear instructions on what you are looking for and what are the criteria for success. There are lots of ways to outsource very cheaply from $200 per month for a full time researcher, but that's something I'll cover later.

Other ways to filter out the information is to plan your research and your time effectively so that you stick to the plan. Always keep a notebook by your computer and if you find yourself being distracted into a new idea, write that down for later research and continue on your original research topic. The key is to exercise that discipline I spoke about earlier. You really must stop yourself when you realise you are moving off topic. It takes practice to become self aware like this, however it's an extremely useful skill to have once you've trained yourself to think this way.

There are also technological ways to filter out results you don't want as well. By using a combination of RSS feed tools and passing them through online filters, you can create your own personal news source or information source that shows you only what you need to see.

One of my personal favourite ways of filtering out social media conversation is by using the RSS sources from Twitter and other social media sites and then by using Yahoo Pipes, we've created some filters to focus in on the conversations and chatter we want to be a part of.

Finding the information has never been easier

Finding the information to help your new online business has never been easier. There are so many different resource sites out there that you can find out just about anything, from customer opinions to hard sales statistics of your competitors.

Here are some sources of information and how they are useful and helpful.

Forums

These are a great source of information from users. Forums are generally created to facilitate discussion amongst people with like-minded interests. You can find online forums on just about any topics from business forums to really obscure ones, like tree pruning.

This is a great place to research the market you are hoping to create your business in. Here you can join in the conversation to find out what your customers' needs really are, and you can also ask questions to help further clarify the need for a solution, or how you will market your products.

Forums are invaluable sources of information generally provided by mavens, people who are keen to discuss the topic, who are somehow invested into finding a solution and sharing it. It's the ground zero for user information.

Question and answer

New to the scene are question and answer sites like Yahoo Answers and some of you might have come across various sites like these. Here you can also ask for information and people will provide their answers to you.

The difference with these sites over forums is that answers are voted on by other members and thus you'll get a general consensus on which is the desired solution or answer to your question.

These kinds of sites also operate in a more real time friendly architecture that lends itself to quicker responses and faster answers to questions, which, after all, is what we as users want.

Social media

Clearly one of the most recent developments is the social media micro update sites, the most famous of which is Twitter. A lot of people think that being on Twitter is all about saying something or tweeting as it's called.

Actually Twitter is an excellent place to be listening to what people are saying. It's a total real time solution to listening in on the conversation currently being had about something. This is an incredibly powerful way to hear about what potential customers are saying in relation to your category.

The speed which messages are delivered are phenomenal. In January 2009, US Airways flight 1549 hit a flock of birds just after take-off causing it to stall its engines. With incredible calmness, Pilot Chesley Sullenberger controlled the powerless Airbus and its 155 passengers towards Manhattan's River Hudson and controlled the crash landing in the water such that there were minimal injuries.

Onlooker Jim Hanrahan broke news of the incident on Twitter, a full 15 minutes before mainstream news media. "I just watched a plane crash in the Hudson," he typed, soon after other tweets followed, including some posting the first images of the crash.

Do you remember the unbelievable tremors felt in the north of England on the night of Wednesday, 27 February 2008? It was the night when a 5.2 magnitude quake hit the area to many people's surprise. Again, the tweet-sphere was awash with news and messages of the event, a full 40 minutes before the first reports were seen on the BBC.

Alexa

Alexa is an incredibly powerful site to use as part of your information-gathering strategy. It allows you to view statistics on your website and also your competitors' websites, which helps you to understand who your visitors are and what your competitors are doing differently.

Here you can find out about visitor demographics, usage statistics, traffic statistics and even site ownership. Be aware that this is basic nature and only reflects the users who have the Alexa toolbar installed. For more advanced information you would need to go elsewhere. I recommend that you use the information on this site as a general guide and overview only.

Article sites

There are lots of sites out there with specific resources and articles on how to use the internet to do business online. These are fantastic places to start reading overviews of how to plan out your internet strategy. They are also great places to learn about the industry you are getting into.

Whois

There are many WHOIS services out there and these are simple services that allow you to find out the owner of a certain domain. By entering the URL details, you'll often find out who owns a site and where they are located. Sometimes you'll also get a contact name, email and telephone number, too.

Online, people are telling you what they want

When it comes to learning about your market and the customers you are wishing to serve, the internet now provides us with the ability to have constant contact with our customers, so there has been a fundamental shift in power towards the customer.

These days, customers tell you exactly what they want and as a business you must provide that solution to them. In the past, before the internet made the conversation so fluid, the customer's voice was relatively unheard. It was very difficult to let the big brands and big companies know what you wanted. The way it was done was always instigated by the company putting out some survey or research to help them communicate with customers better. This was how it was done in the past, now customers have the ability to voice their needs all the time, globally and without the consent of the company.

This means that you must really listen in on the social conversation to gauge what you must do to provide a valuable solution, or what you need to do to improve a current solution.

Markets are telling you what the market needs through tools that can all be found online. Below I'm going to talk about four of my favourite ways to gauge the market.

Google for solutions

Google is the agony aunt of the world. It's essentially a solution finder for any problem that you have. Think about the fact that whenever you are searching for something, you are actually looking for a solution to a problem.

By searching on your topic you can get a good idea of the marketplace online as you look through the Google results and other information around the Google screen.

Of course you have the search results that show you the competition. If there are other people already in the search engine results providing solutions similar to what you are providing, then that is a good sign that a market already exists. If no one is selling a solution then you need to think about whether the market for your solution really exists.

There are other indicators of market size on Google. On the right there is what's known as Google Adwords. AdWords ads are displayed along with search results when someone searches Google using one of your keywords. Ads also appear under 'Sponsored links' in the side column of a search page and may also appear in additional positions above the free search results. In order to place an ad in these positions, people place bids for clicks, also known as a Pay-Per-Click system. Pay per click (PPC) is an internet advertising model used on websites, where advertisers pay their host only when the ad is clicked. With search engines, advertisers typically bid on keyword phrases relevant to their target market.

This means that if you did a search on your topic, and you see adverts on the Adwords sections, it's a good sign that there is a market because other people are bidding on those keywords, so it must mean that they are making money or determined that money can be made from this keyword term.

If there are too many adverts here, it would indicate an extremely competitive market. You can also gauge competitiveness through Google's Adwords site, which allows you to see the bid values on key terms in your industry. In certain high competition industries, I've seen click values all the way up to $60 per click, so this is definitely something to take into account when researching your market place online.

Another way to see what the marketplace is doing is by looking at the bottom of a Google search results page and seeing what the related searches are to the term you've typed in. Here you'll see a list of the most type of searches by other people, allowing you to see other interesting trends in what people are looking for.

As an example, when I do a search for 'car insurance' the related searches at the bottom of the page show me the following additional search terms:

- auto insurance quotes

- cheap car insurance

- compare car insurance

- farmers car insurance

- car insurance questions

- car insurance reviews

- car insurance ratings

- car insurance Wikipedia

This tells me that the market is looking for quotes; that they want cheaper car insurance and they are interested in comparison sites to get the best deal. What's also interesting is that these search results have also highlighted an interesting potential sub-niche to me that I might not have thought about if I were a car insurance supplier. It would seem people are looking for farmers' car insurance, a very specific micro-niche of the car insurance niche.

YouTube for services

If you are providing a service, besides Google, YouTube is an excellent way to determine the marketplace because you can see if people are looking for video help regarding the services you are providing. If you are providing a service, you are providing a solution to some problem. Typically, people will want to find out whether there is help online and more and more people are looking on YouTube to find the information themselves.

You'll always find videos providing a solution to the problem your service tries to solve; however the indicator whether there is a need for this will be in the number of views the videos get. Another indicator is also the number of videos around the topic of your service; however the greatest indicator by far is the view count.

For example, if you were a children's party organizer and you wanted to find out whether adding a face painting service would be beneficial, you could use YouTube to see if other people have online video tutorials about it and how many people have viewed it. I searched for "children's face painting tutorial" and I saw a video about painting a dinosaur face which had 65,222 views and another video on painting a butterfly which had 178,534 views. This is a clear indication of a market for this, which would mean that adding the face painting service would be a good move for your children's party business.

eBay for products

If you are developing a product and wanted to see the competition for similar products on the market, a great place to look is on eBay. Here you can see what other people are supplying and at what price. It's a fantastic way to research the market for your products and also to see what other solutions are out there.

It gives you some ideas on what prices people are paying and also what sells well. A products category that sells well will have lots of pages of results on eBay, whereas something that doesn't sell will have very few options.

Market Samurai for market overview

Market Samurai is one of my personal favourite tools for doing market research and analysis. It's a software tool that you download onto your computer and it uses connections to various online data sources to gather and then correlate the data into useful statistic sets.

Most notably it gathers Google keyword data and then does a cross comparison of the results to give you useful information about the marketplace you are intending to enter. It has some great features that provide a much clearer indication of potential market size for any given keyword. The Online Commercial Intent (OCI) statistic is particularly interesting because it gives an indicator of the chances that someone searching for a keyword is looking to buy, as opposed to browsing for information. The higher the figure, the more likely they want to buy.

Workshop 7: Creating Your Own Curriculum

This is the first workshop that involves some internet research. It's obvious by now that there are things you will need to learn before you can get started, however it's not just as simple as reading it; you need to find out what your learning strategy is and work with that. Some people like to learn through doing, some people learn by reading, some people learn by watching and listening.

1) Think about three different times when you succeeded at learning something easily and rapidly, then consider the following:

   a. What was the method of learning?

   b. Why do you think you learnt particularly easily on this occasion?

   c. What told you the lessons learnt were truly part of your knowledge?

2) What do you need to learn now in order to move forward:

   a. For the first month – what is most important, right now, in order to get started?

   b. For the first 6 months – What is most important to get traction and momentum?

   c. For the first year – what is most important to ensure success?

3) How many hours per week can you devote to learning?

4) Now search online for learning resources and create a document that you can refer to during your year that contains all these resources. Plan out the topics and timescale according to the answers you've given above, making sure the learning mechanism is the same as your answers to question 1.

Congratulations, you have now created your online learning curriculum for the next 12 months.

Notes

SECRET 8

It's Not Just for Geeks!

Despite what people say and what you think about being able to do business online, you don't actually have to be technically minded in order to make it work. In fact, I would even go so far as to say that it might be a hindrance being technically minded because you might leave yourself closed to all the options available for doing things more easily.

There are more free-to-use systems than ever before and this wasn't even possible 5 years ago, so technology has really come a long way since I first started out. When I got started, you really did need a certain level of technical competence to build an online business, however there are plenty of new services available today that make life a lot easier.

Systems ahoy

These systems, that are literally everywhere, can do all sorts of things for you; all you need to have is a clear mind ready to learn. They are not difficult to learn, but you must have patience and do the step as instructed, otherwise you might cause yourself more pain than is really necessary.

There is also an art to finding the systems and filtering out those that don't work. Most systems will have some sort of a trial period that will allow you to test it and see if it works for you. Note some systems are designed for the more technically minded, so be specific about what you are looking for.

Content management systems

Content management systems are probably the best resource that you can get your hands on because they really empower you to self administer your website and update it as you see fit.

The main advantage of these systems is that they allow people with zero technical knowledge to operate and run a highly complex website. We have clients today running these systems, which only a few years ago wouldn't have been possible. In fact, one of our clients is a Bedouin tribesman out in the Wadi Rum desert in Jordan and he has a site to promote the jeep tours they run from the desert. The solution allows him now to upload new photos, add new blog content and provides a place for his clients to comment as well.

There are also many other benefits that these systems offer as well, all of which serve just to empower you even more. Here are some additional benefits:

- Automated templates – standard design templates can be automatically applied to new and existing content, allowing the appearance of all content to be changed from one central place. This means you can update your site design very easily and cheaply.

- Scalable expansion – it's geared for growth so you can safely invest and know you have something that has the ability to grow as your business expands.

- Easily editable content – it is much easier and quicker to edit and manipulate content. Most systems include 'what you see is what you get' (WYSIWYG) editing tools allowing non-technical people to create and edit content.

- Scalable feature sets – it's extremely easy to adapt and add new functionality to the sites at later stages.

- Web standards upgrades – due to a large number of people updating the core systems, these CMS systems adhere to web standards with regular updates.

- Workflow management – allows multiple people to contribute to the site

- Document management – allows documents to be centralised and controlled

- Content syndication – most systems produce RSS and Atom data feeds, which are excellent for releasing content and for SEO purposes.

- Multilingual

So you can see, these are awesome systems and I want to highlight three that are considered to be the best ones available today.

Wordpress

I think just about everyone has heard of Wordpress by now. Out of a research study of 1 million of the biggest websites, over 13% use Wordpress as its platform now.

Wordpress first appeared in 2003 as the creation of Matt Mullenweg and Mike Little and was one of the first CMS systems to allow user templating and the re-arrangement of widgets or modules to suit the site's design.

It is known primarily as a blogging platform which features integrated link management; a search engine-friendly, clean permalink structure;

the ability to assign multiple categories to articles and support for tagging of posts and articles. Automatic filters are also included, providing standardized formatting and styling of text in articles. Wordpress also supports the Trackback and Pingback standards for displaying links to other sites that have them linked to a post or article. Finally, Wordpress has a rich plug-in architecture that allows users and developers to extend its functionality beyond the features that come as part of the base install.

The Wordpress system is excellent for sites that are focused on delivering blog style information. Whether that is in the form of news articles, reviews or constant updates, the system is really setup for this fast-paced information delivery.

From a technical point of view, it is by far the easiest to install and maintain and module updates can be upgraded from within the system itself, without the need to download any update files.

Joomla!

Another great CMS that I've used, launched in 2005, is Joomla! which, within its first year of release was downloaded over 2.5 million times. It currently has over 6000 commercial plug-ins and the name itself is derived from an anglicised spelling of a Swahili word *jumla* meaning 'all together' or 'as a whole'.

Joomla! is a cross-platform system which means you can install it on most standard hosting systems; its feature-rich standard setup makes it a great choice for people working on a budget and wanting to develop and maintain a website themselves.

Joomla! is written in PHP, uses object-oriented programming (OOP) techniques and software design patterns, stores data in a MySQL database and includes features such as page caching, RSS feeds, printable versions of pages, news flashes, blogs, polls, search and support for language internationalisation.

Overall it is an excellent system, however from a scalability point of view, tests have shown that Drupal is a better choice for growth and potential large-scale deployments.

Drupal

Interestingly, Drupal has been around longer than Wordpress, making its appearance back in 2001 as a message board, but later being redesigned as a CMS system. Another interesting fact about Drupal is that it is a community project, which means people from all over the world contribute to the development of the system, bringing the best talent together to create a CMS that is extremely powerful, yet simple at the same time.

Its reach is evident; as of July 2010, over 7.2 million sites use Drupal as a platform, including companies, non-profits, schools and even governments. Some recognisable brands to use this as their core website include MTV UK, *The Economist* and even the US White House.

Some of the key features of Drupal include: localisation, auto-update notifications, high levels of user configurability and the support it has for Windows developers as well.

Drupal also has just over 6,000 free modules to extend the system's functionality. In fact, the system is designed in a way like a blank canvas that allows users to really exercise their creative input to develop a website from scratch, using just plug-ins and templates.

I love Drupal, I must admit that this is by far my favourite due to its adaptive nature and how unbelievably powerful it is as a tool. I've often wondered that if this solution was available to me 10 years ago, how much more I might have been able to achieve. These systems are truly empowering to new entrepreneurs.

Ecommerce solutions

Whilst the content management systems are great for website development, if you need to create an online store as well, there are better tailored systems for ecommerce design specifically to sell products. These are called online store management systems and below are a few to choose from.

osCommerce

This is an open source system developed in PHP and it's available free under a general public license. It was started back in 2000 in Germany by Harold Ponce de Leon as The Exchange Project and is reported to have around 12,700 live websites using this system. One of the criticisms made about this system is the security around sql injection-type hacks.

To date there are over 6,400 add-ons available for free to customize osCommerce Online Merchant online stores that help increase sales.

Magento

Relatively new, Magento was launched in 2008 and it is developed by a company called Varien, which currently employs over 180 people. Their ecommerce platform is aimed more towards the small-to-mid-size business market and is pitched as a mid-tier system.

Magento supports the installation of additional modules for added functionality directly through a web-based administration system, as well as applicable themed templates.

Zen Cart

Zen Cart is a branch of osCommerce and the split happened in 2003 with Zen Cart making a fundamental architecture change to its system and increasing the core functionality.

It also introduced a template system at the time not available on osCommerce and also had facilities that could track and sell gift vouchers as well as digital downloads.

Zen Cart's default installation provides everything needed to maintain a shopping cart web site. Products, pricing, shipping, newsletters, sales etc can be managed by you through the administration area. The shopping cart is set up to receive payments from major credit cards via your own choice of numerous available payment gateway services, some built-in or easily added with free add-ons.

The Zen Cart software is easily customisable to whatever your needs but it does depend on the skills and resources you have available. Only minimal skills are required to get started; however more advanced customisations may require stronger knowledge of CSS, HTML, and maybe PHP or maybe even MySQL, depending on your unique requirements.

This is a powerful solution and it's the one I've chosen to specialise in for my company. We chose this one because it is highly adaptable and there is a strong development framework and developer community, which ensures that there are constant updates as web technology continues to advance.

PrestaShop

This solution was launched in August 2007 and it too is aimed at small-to-medium sized businesses with built-in payment facilities for Google checkout, PayPal or Payments Pro via the API, however further payment modules are only available commercially.

Whilst the system has been translated into 40 different languages, currently full support is only available in the English and French versions of the software. Because it is a more recent system, it uses AJAX technology extensively in the admin panel, whilst other modules can be added to provide more functionality to the shop front.

This, too, is an incredibly powerful platform and some of the benefits on the shop front include: special deals (price reductions, gift vouchers), 'free shipping' offers, order out-of-stock items, package tracking, PDF customer invoice and Affiliate programme.

The choice is yours to make

As you can see, there is plenty of choice there and every solution has fantastic benefits. What's key to understand here is that it really is so easy to create a site once you have these systems installed and some of them are so easy to install that it really doesn't take any technical knowledge to do it.

For example, the Wordpress installation is about three steps and takes 5 minutes. It's so foolproof you can't even go wrong with it.

Exercise your creativity to make things happen

Creating an online business that succeeds is not about being the best technically; it's about being the best creatively. This is because it really does take a creative mind in order to develop a genuine online business that not only has real value, but also has all the right technology behind it to deliver your chosen solution.

You have to be flexible in your mind in order to think around problems that appear. When I was doing my first photo shoot, about 30 minutes before the actual shooting was due to begin, my radio triggers broke and I had a real problem; that radio trigger controlled my speedlight and I needed the light control my speedlight offered to achieve the results I was looking for.

I needed to work around the problem; immediately I went to a nearby photography store, only to find that it didn't open for another 20 minutes. Frantically I had to devise a solution, so I first attempted to fix the radio trigger with some solder and tape. It didn't work. Luckily the shoot was delayed which gave me time to revisit the photography shop. Still, though, they didn't have what I needed but instead I did find a corded trigger cable that could to the trick. The only restraint was that it was now non-wireless which restricted my movement; however it was a solution and I had to take it.

In the end, we managed to complete the shoot successfully, which just goes to show that thinking creatively both artistically and laterally is required to get over obstacles in your path to success.

Multiple routes to a goal

As you've read, there are plenty of CMS systems for you to choose from, so creativity comes into play because you'll need to exercise it to imagine what you are setting out to achieve, in order to decide which system works for your vision.

Just as with satellite navigation systems, there are multiple ways to get from A to B, so from a technical perspective, if you aren't technically minded, you need to start thinking creatively and laterally to chart those new routes when you encounter a problem in developing your website.

Whether you choose to do things yourself or find other people to do it, there are always many ways to get to the same place. Particularly when you look online, there are growing numbers of people providing services at affordable costs, which gives you a plethora of choice.

In my company, we've recently spent 5 months developing a system of charting that we were going to use via Excel spreadsheets to show statistical analysis on a real-time basis. However, once we neared the end of the project, it was having some real problems making the real-time connections, so we had to quickly research and devise a new way to represent the data.

Within a week we managed to find another solution online and it was free to use. We discovered an XML charting solution that allowed us to display this statistical data in real time on our company intranet. This was an even more powerful solution than our initial solution and it only took 1 week to implement, versus the 5 months we spent doing it ourselves.

Often I have found that initial plans always develop into something more at a later stage, so keep your creative mind at work and always explore multiple options to solve a problem.

Creative solutions are everywhere

Like I've already mentioned, there are lots of fantastic services online to help, and here is a list of my favourite creative solutions to help your new business to develop and thrive.

Animoto.com

This is a fantastic place that will allow you to create a short promotional video with little to no expertise in video editing. The system creates incredibly sophisticated video edits that would otherwise take a professional at least 4-5 hours to create.

It takes your video clips and images and creates a video with music background and text overlay within minutes. It's really an incredible service and highly recommended.

Fiverr.com

This is a unique website which has the base premise that everything on the site costs $5. You can find all sorts of creative solutions here to suit your needs, from background designs, to social media marketing help.

There's everything you can think of on this site, even bizarre ones like "I will write and sing a song for your loved one with my acoustic 12 string guitar for $5" or "I will dance to an entire song of your choice in a hot dog costume for $5".

99Designs.com

This is a great place to get professional logos and designs done. What's unique about this site is the way it works. What you do is place up a contest for your logo and multiple designers will submit their entries for the contest.

It runs over several days and throughout the process you feedback to the design group and watch as the tweaks come in. A typical project will end up with over 100 designs to choose from and only the winner will get paid. This is great for extremely high quality work, however you will have to pay for this service and it's not cheap.

Survey Monkey

If you thought doing market research was difficult, welcome to Survey Monkey, which allows you to conduct polls quite easily. Through their simple interface you create your poll questions and then all you have to do is send out a link through your networks to start getting feedback and analysis.

It's extremely powerful and it's totally free. Consider that only a few years ago, this kind of market research was extremely costly to run, now you can get all that information with careful planning and a free polling service.

Adobe Kuler

If you're stuck thinking about what colours work well together, then Adobe's Kuler website is the site go to all the time to figure out what my next colour scheme is going to be, whether for a project or a new bedroom I might be painting! This website has colour systems programmed in so that you can pick a single colour and choose a colour model and it will start to match complementary colours.

I don't know anywhere else to go for this, and after all colour is Adobe's business!

Moo.com

If you need customized stationery and business cards, Moo.com offers fantastic resources for uploading and creating a set of stationery with photos or uploaded graphics.

The great thing is that it connects with Flickr, so it really makes uploads and choosing your cards really easy. The ordering process is quite simple and the cards are very high quality.

Again it's very easy to use their website and you'll have a set of new cards in less time than you can imagine.

There is always a way to automate

Once you've found the technical solutions which work for you, and you've begun to use them and learnt the details of how to run your site efficiently and effectively, the last step is to find ways to automate and take yourself out of the equation so you can stick with the creative tasks that help to develop your business further.

Creativity comes into place here for you to think about how you can automate a particular process within your business. The power of automation is fairly self-explanatory, since everybody's time is so valuable.

When I started out creating websites and particularly my core project in the early days, I really needed to find automation solutions fast because I was a solopreneur, which meant that I simply didn't have the time to do all the repetitive maintenance and creative tasks. Instead, I developed ways to automate and this allowed me to grow the website substantially. How else could a single person maintain, run and grow a site that had over 10,000 pages of unique content? Today, that site is almost 80% fully automated.

One of my personal favourite technologies to appear is the RSS feed technology that allows all data to be represented in a standard format.

RSS, which stands for Really Simple Syndication, is a family of web feed formats used to publish frequently updated works such as blog entries, news headlines, audio and video. This allows you to publish your content on autopilot and also empowers readers to subscribe to your content with other mechanisms like RSS readers and even directly, in some email software.

Using external systems to build your business

Remember, you don't have to have a website in order to build an online business, so you could potentially skip the whole website part altogether.

There are so many facilitator services on the internet that I know many people have built an internet business on top of other people's systems without the need for their own website.

Selling on eBay

My number one choice for people selling products who want to test the market before having their own website is doing it through eBay. eBay offer an incredible selling platform and many businesses online and offline have used it to deliver massive returns to their business.

Founded in 1995, it was originally an auction website where people could bid for items to try to obtain them at a lower than retail cost. When eBay introduced the 'Buy it Now' option to item listings, it created an opportunity for retailers to also get into the market place and deliver their goods to the customer cheaply and immediately, without waiting for the auction to be over.

There have been many business success stories on eBay and there are literally thousands of people who have become financially free selling on eBay.

One notable person to mention here is Adam Ginsberg who has written books on how to buy and sell on eBay. He started out cynical about eBay but still back in 2001 he placed a pool table to sell and he sold it with ease. As a result he continued to engage in eBay sales, expanding his online business and eventually closing his physical store. By the end of 2002 Ginsberg had been named as eBay's 'number-one new seller' and he is said to have sold over $20 million worth of products through the online service.

In another story closer to home in the UK, just a little over 5 years ago, Amanda and Matt Clarkson found themselves broke. Matt was doing a dead-end carpenting job and Amanda sold pies from the back of a white van. Today they live a life of yachts, fast cars and designer brands after having made over £8 million selling goods on eBay.

The inspiration came when Matt was working one day at a wealthy person's mansion and whilst having a break, he watched a yacht pull up to the pier. From curiosity he asked the man how he made so much money and the man responded that he created some software for the internet.

Feeling inspired, despite having no computer knowledge, he started to find things to sell on eBay and he started with things around his house from CDs, DVDs and books to anything they could see on their shelves.

It wasn't long before they found that they were making £400 a week profit from things they didn't want. The biggest lesson they learnt was that you must not assume what people would want to buy. Later he sold some camping gear and because it sold well, he investigated further and found that he could buy direct from manufacturers in China, unbranded; armed with credit card in hand, he purchased £5000 worth of camping equipment and managed to make a profit of £4000.

Their initial targets was just to make £1000 a month, however that soon spiralled and as the business began to expand, they reinvested all the profits back into buying stock and investing in education, spending thousands on courses on internet business and marketing.

From a complete standing start, they were turning over £24,000 in eight months. Now they make over £750k a year, but the best part is that they only spend 10 hours a week working. Today most of their goods are homeware items like pots, pans and kitchen goods.

In 2010, there were 127 eBay shops in the UK that had a reported turnover of over £1m; you can understand how it is now a thriving hub of activity for small businesses.

You can also sell goods through Amazon Shops, though having looked at the differences I would recommend eBay as the platform to start with for new entrepreneurs. Although Amazon Shops offer the same kind of selling system, there are fundamental differences in the way Amazon operates, which changes the way you would be selling from eBay. In general there are tougher guidelines and competition for higher levels of customer service on Amazon, which generally means it's geared more towards established mid-to-large scale sellers.

Selling wholesale

If you are manufacturing products, then there's no better way to reach even more customers by offering your services than through Alibaba. com. As I've mentioned before, Alibaba makes it easy for importers and exporters to connect through their global trade platform; in addition Alibaba offers a transaction-based wholesale platform on the global site (AliExpress) geared for smaller buyers seeking fast shipment of small quantities of goods.

This means that you don't need a website to display your products; you can just create an account on Alibaba and sell direct to people in different countries.

The system is very easy to use and it offers amazing flexibility for manufacturing companies to do business online. It is especially relevant because a lot of manufacturing companies don't have highly skilled internet-savvy employees. The system gives them the ability to upload images of their products and enter all the details of what they can offer, with absolute ease and efficiency.

Selling services as an outsourcer

This is a great way to start off building some capital if you don't want to have a website. There are many ways in which you can outsource your workload as I've mentioned before, however have you considered becoming an outsource provider yourself?

There are many benefits to this. It could allow you to test the market for your services and your price point. It also means you don't have to have a website because you can sell your services through websites like Elance, Odesk or PeoplePerHour.

You could use these jobs as a way of fine tuning your service before you offer it on your own website later, or you can simply just run a business as a freelancer offering services to other people. The way most of these sites work is that the more jobs you complete successfully, the better your ranking and that leads to more successful job bids and being able to charge higher prices.

When you start with a new account here, you'll have to obviously compete on price initially, however once you've done several jobs at low cost, and built up a reputation and feedback, you can start to really go for better jobs with high rates of return.

This is also a great way to fund an idea. For example, if you want to build a business that requires a substantial lead time and planning and investment, you could, in the meantime, take on some freelance work to help to build up the capital to fund your core idea.

My company uses a lot of these services and we now have several writers on our books that write on specific topics. They are creating a new source of income and possibly working full time on it if they are good at what they do. Otherwise it is still a great source of additional income to supplement your main job income, all great for building up your investment capital for your big business idea.

Workshop 8: Creating a Technical Strategy

Now that you have a better idea about your solution, your vision, what you need to learn and where you need to invest your resources, it's time to plan a strategy to make all that work online.

Here are some important questions you need to answer to move forward now:

1) Which type of online solution do you think will work for your business?

   a. Do you need a website?

   b. Are you going to market just via social networks?

2) What are the objectives of your website?

   a. Is the main objective to sell a service or product, promote an idea, get a phone call, complete a quotation form, etc?

   b. Who is going to build it for you?

    c. How much time or money are you going to invest?

3) What creative assets will you need?

    a. How are you going to get them?

    b. What style will your brand take on board?

4) Which kind of websites do your prospects visit?

    a. What attracts them to those sites?

    b. What is the website doing that converts visitors into buyers?

5) How likely are your prospects going to be to buy your solution online?

    a. What are the challenges in converting them to an online purchaser?

    b. Is there a maximum price your prospects will be willing to pay to buy direct online before they need to speak to someone first?

6) How are you going to deliver your solution online to them?

    a. Is there something you need to ship?

    b. How will the ordering process work online?

    c. Will you offer online payment methods?

Once you've answered these, you should start to get a good idea about how your technical strategy will work.

Notes

SECRET 9

Anyone can be Famous

Part of creating a successful business online is all about the fame. Whether this is personal fame for yourself as a brand, or making your product or service famous, you need to be able to raise the profile of your solution in order to gain trust, credibility and ultimately sales.

What is great about using the internet to market your business and grow your fame is that it is much cheaper to do now than ever before. You can become extremely influential and 'web' famous, even before you become more widely known.

There are numerous examples of people becoming extremely popular online that led eventually to massive success overall. I've already mentioned Michelle Phan of YouTube makeup fame. There is also the singer Lily Allen who first became famous on MySpace by recording her own songs and making them available publicly online. After music scouts spotted the massive number of views on her MySpace profile, they approached her with a deal and her debut record sold over 2.6 million copies.

Another example is the recent meteoric rise of Justin Bieber as a singer-songwriter after being discovered on YouTube, he was signed to Raymond Braun Media Group where his debut release, My World, went platinum in the USA.

There are two things to be clear on before proceeding with this section. First thing to understand is that you won't get web famous unless you actually have something valuable to offer. No amount of internet marketing will get you famous if what you're offering is rubbish. The examples above all delivered massive value to their prospects.

The second thing to note is that you must define what famous means for you in your chosen industry. You can't expect to be celebrity famous if you are working in the pharmaceutical industry. You need to identify other people of fame in your industry and define what it really means to be famous before you can set your goal to be famous in that industry. After all, you couldn't hit a football into a goal without first knowing what a goal looks like.

The importance of being an influencer

In every industry there are people that seem to have all the opportunities come to them. In fact, they don't ever have to go out selling, they are already pre-sold. So this inner circle is where you want to be.

These opportunities are often the best ones in the market as well. They are the ones that everybody is chasing. When you are the influencer in your industry, you'll be presented with these all the time and your only question will be how you make the most of them, or whether they're something that you should take up.

In fact, one big lesson you'll have to learn to do is how to say, 'no'. In this influential position, new business ventures will come your way almost like a magnet drawing iron filings to it. I fell into this 'no' trap early on when I hadn't learnt the lesson about opportunity cost versus pay off. I agreed to help several new business ventures that seemed to have lots of potential, however the time I spent help those people didn't pay off and I learnt a great lesson about it.

I was approached to help a start-up cosmetics company to establish a brand and develop a product. Even though right from the start it was evident that there was plenty of passion in the individual, they lacked a vast array of basic business skills to even have their company set up in the right way. Instead of spending our consulting time developing the product, most of it was spent teaching the basics of business. As I've mentioned in an earlier chapter, these are skills you've got to learn right from the beginning.

A few years ago I was also approached by a business contact who wanted to propose a merger of several affiliate businesses into one larger organisation. There were four parties involved of which I was one, and the idea was that as a larger organisation, we could pool resources and also have greater leverage on the affiliate programmes. That deal never happened, however it only came about because I was perceived as an influential person in that industry.

Key influencers also hear about deals before anyone else because they are well connected and trusted, so people will gossip and tell them stories. This can often lead to great new opportunities as well.

When someone is thinking about a deal, they will think of the social connector first. When I had begun conversations with an events promoter in 2010, through my introductions I rapidly became a person of influence as I introduced many people to this event; because of that, I'm now getting to hear the inner circle conversations which are not only interesting, but can lead to serious opportunities later down the line.

Spotting the influencers

Everyone knows who the inner circle is, so spotting them generally isn't difficult. There are a number of ways to identify these people. If you are out and about attending networking events or seminars, you'll start to notice that some people tend to show up in person, or in conversation a lot of the time. Begin to take notice of these people as it's clear that if they are around and being talked about, they are a key person in the inner circle.

Another great way to distinguish these people is that they have great online profiles across the board. Not only are they highly active on social networks, they will often have their own company website and in some cases even their own profile website which is when you know they are an extremely high profile individual.

There is something to be aware of, and that is that online, some people are highly active, however, they are not necessarily influential people. Some people just like to be active for active's sake. You need to do your due diligence. It's all part of the equation, so seeing an active person on social networks is just the start.

Influencers also have high levels of branding. Whether they are branding their company or themselves, you'll often find that the key people have great branding. This means their message is congruent across all their online media, and also echoes across to their offline media like business cards, flyers and literature.

Getting congruent through branding

Since we've moved onto the branding aspect, this in my opinion is one of the most important activities to gain internet fame, and it is often the most poorly implemented part of most start-up companies' strategy.

The key message here is that the branding and what it represents must be congruent across everything you do. This means everything, from your online social media, to your website, to your business card design and even to your personal fashion style. It's really important to understand that as the founder of your business, your entire image and character is part of the branding equation, so taking a step back and analysing yourself is vital to success.

Social media spider web

Remember that we've discussed the core message of your business brand, so this message must match that of all of your social media and social networking sites. You need to make sure that the message is the same on Facebook as it is on Twitter. You need to ensure that there isn't mixed messages and cross communication because that will dilute what you stand for and then you'll become unmemorable.

The best way that I've discovered to get this single message out to many networks at once is to use a distribution and management service for social networks. What these services do is allow you to register and enter details of your social networks into them. By their use of technology and linking to these sites, you can enter your message once on these sites and they will spread the message to all your networks for you. Sites like Hootsuite and Seesmic provide such capabilities and also help you to visualize what is happening in your social web.

By connecting everything together such that it is a single congruent system of messaging, you are creating your own social media spider web. When a fly lands on a spider web, the spider will know about it no matter where it is, or where the fly is. In the same manner, your interconnected social media system is like a spider web. When you throw a message out to it, you want everyone else to flock to it, no matter where they are online.

Harness the power of conversation

To gain great traction online and develop that fame to get you to the inner circle, you must develop the skill to communicate effectively and to increase your interaction with other people in your social networks.

A few things to do that may seem simple, but are absolutely necessary, are to provide a place online for people to interact to promote conversation in the topics you discuss. Although sites like Twitter and Facebook provide great facilities to have this conversation, I would still recommend that you try to gain that traction on your own blog.

There are a number of reasons why having a separate blog is preferable, firstly because being able to control the conversation is key when it comes to dealing with people who are out to cause problems for you via your social networks. This can rapidly escalate if measures are taken quickly, and on your own site you can take those down with total control. Even with Facebook's privacy and degree of control, there will be times when you can't do anything about a rogue comment. Secondly, if you have a separate blog, it gives you just a little bit more kudos because the perception will be that you care enough to have a dedicated blog on your subject. This lends itself well to marking you out as influential.

When you provide a place of your own for people to interact, it also earns you great search engine credit when it spiders your site and sees that your blog is active with comments appearing regularly. This will serve you well on search engine listings.

Also on external blog sites, you can provide even more social bookmarking options that places like Twitter or Facebook don't provide. Your users could be from anywhere in the world and they are most likely to have lots of different preferences in the way they surf online. Some might prefer using Bebo as their social network, or perhaps some people like to use DIGG or Stumbleupon to bookmark your pages; what's vital to understand is that by providing these options, you'll get better reach across the entire internet.

Facebook will share only internally within Facebook, and Twitter is the same. Having the comments and blogs on your own site will allow you to use a service like ADDthis which will allow your visitors to share on over 300 different social networks, some of which you might not even have been familiar with, but are extremely popular in other countries.

Here's just a few names of these popular services: Digg, Stumbleupon, Mixx, Orkut, Google Buzz, Myspace, Delicious, Blogger, Vkontakte, Gmail, Reddit, Lifestream, Linkedin, Meneame, Baidu.

The effect that this has, when your message is strong and comes across in every online element, is that you can create a viral marketing effect with just people's voices alone. Your customers and visitors become your best fans and through them, your message will spread much wider and further than your own reach.

The success story that I think illustrates this magnificently is that of the Zappos.com success through the innovative strategy that was used to realign the company message. Through their strong branding ensuring there was a singular message about their incredible customer service, they create raving fans out of their customers and that message was spread by word of mouth alone.

A couple of the stories I've heard help to reiterate how dedicated to this message they are, and how every team member in the company understands this. The first story is about their tours that allow customers to go visit their offices whilst in Las Vegas. Their tours are completely free and I once heard one customer speak about this. They would pick people up from the airport, drive them to the office to tour and during the tour they could speak to anyone in the company. At the end of the tour they gave the customer gifts from their store, so many gifts that he couldn't physically carry them all, so instead they just shipped them to his home. Then they took him to his hotel in a limousine. The experience was so impressive that this person had to tell everyone about it and that in itself is the best marketing you could have.

In another story, the CEO was out with friends after a business meeting; they got home to their hotel late that evening, but they still wanted to get a pizza delivered! They didn't know what to do, so one of the friends suggested phoning Zappos' customer service to test them, whilst the CEO was present, just for fun.

They called the Zappos customer service and asked them if they knew anywhere where they could get a pizza delivered at 2am to their hotel room. The member of customer service reiterated a few times that they were an online shoe store, in case the caller wasn't aware, but still ended up finding some places from an online search and helping the callers to find a place that would deliver. The company culture of customer service was so strong that no matter what the enquiry was, they would deal with it.

You can see that providing a talking point like these will certainly increase the chances of social communication playing a key part in your overall online branding strategy.

Becoming a public person

Part of being famous is being in the public eye, even if it's only within your industry. Many people create businesses online and forget about the impersonal nature of the internet, thinking that they can get away with just logos, websites and their computer screens, however, I think it's even more important to project a public image when you are developing an online business.

People don't do businesses with websites or internet companies, they do business with other people, so making it personal and profiling yourself as the founder is massively important. You're going to have to face those fears about putting yourself on the pedestal.

Remember that the person sitting at home or at work is mostly going to be visiting your online media by themselves, so treat them as if you are talking to them one to one. It is because you are online that they will need to see a real person behind the company you are setting up. This is because they need to feel that they can trust you, that you are 'real' and credible.

Like it or not, they will begin to search out your online profile, and unless you are a secret agent with a double identity, they will find you on Facebook or Linkedin, or some other social networking site, because this is part of their natural due diligence.

When they find you, you need to be presentable. You need to live your brand. Personal image and style is going to come into play here because it must reiterate your branding. You must at all times be representing yourself and your brand in the best possible light. You never know when you'll get snapped on camera or meet a new potential customer. It's better to be prepared than to look completely incongruent with what you are selling.

You might be thinking right now how ridiculous that I'm telling you to re-evaluate your personal style. I'm telling you it's true, it's vital. All you have to do is to look at someone like Richard Branson who has a certain style, and you know it reflects how he does business and his Virgin brand. It reflects it all the time. In fact, if you look at the various successful people online, from the world of celebrity, business and sports, you'll find that they all have congruent styles the whole time they are living, even going to the supermarket.

They understand something: that they need to be recognised. By accepting that they are a public figure, they can embrace that position and act from a point of excellence and congruence.

It's quite easy to get an image consultant to help you craft your image so that it mirrors what your brand is about and how you will go about your life with this ethos in mind, living your brand every waking moment.

The final part of image is to always have your biography written up in varying lengths so that it's always easy to send to people and to copy into social media profiles. Also, as you begin to gain traction in your market place, you'll be asked to do interviews and perhaps guest writing on other people's websites, so having a ready-made biography that is in line with your brand message will save you time and energy.

The megaphone internet

Imagine the internet as being the biggest megaphone on the planet and that anything you say can be multiplied many times over, just as much as your customer's voice is also on the end of a megaphone.

Online, everyone has a voice which can be heard anywhere in the world. Think about that for a second and imagine how profound that really is. You can write something on your blog, and it can be read by literally anyone on the planet whether on a computer or on a mobile device. Think about what that means for you and your business.

Everyone has a TV channel

Not only do they have a voice, you can also have your own broadcasting channel for free. YouTube is now the second largest search engine in the world. People are looking for video content more than ever, and you can create your own channel for free and start to communicate your value through the medium of online video.

The use of video is an important element in the whole branding process and in the entire value of the company you are setting up. A common problem online is that customers feel they don't know who to trust, so having video content of yourself communicating your value and what your company is about will accelerate the rapport building and enable you to establish greater degrees of trust with your potential customers.

Having online videos shows that you are prepared to put yourself out there, and customers can relate to that. It helps to develop credibility as well, giving viewers a chance to listen to your advice or information, and make their own assessment whether they want to deal with you more.

You are in fact killing two birds with one stone because as well as developing that trust and credibility you are also pre-screening or pre-qualifying your customers, so people who end up working with you or getting in touch with you after viewing your videos are much more likely to buy.

Reaching millions from your toilet

As I've said on numerous occasions, the power of the internet is such that you can be sitting on your toilet and still be communicating with anyone and everyone at the same time. You might want to keep off the video and audio though and just stick to text communication!

Seriously though, the mobile device market has made the internet accessible to everyone on the move. People are actively online, checking their social networking sites, 'tweeting', buying goods, looking for restaurants, writing emails, taking photos and uploading them live. They are doing all these things and even more, all the time, everywhere on the planet.

What this means for you in terms of manufacturing fame is that you can be in constant communication with your audience, and that means whenever you have a great idea, you can instantly share it with your network, even if you are on the toilet!

Joking aside, this is actually an incredibly important aspect of communication at present. The instant factor has become something that people are following. The success of Twitter is due to the fact that the messages are in real-time, meaning people can read people they follow and feel like they are connected to them at a deeper more personal level.

Your customers will also want this from you, so being timely and talking online is something that you'll just have to get used to doing constantly. It needs to become a part of your lifestyle.

Workshop 9: Making Yourself Internet Famous

As I've said, becoming internet famous involves you taking yourself seriously and putting yourself in the limelight. To be influential is to be public, no one ever became successful without putting themselves out there, so now is your chance to begin that journey.

1) List the key people in your industry whom you would happily do a joint venture with. At this early stage in your business, you just want to make them aware of you and begin to show up on their radar.

   a. Get in touch with each one of them and just start a friendly conversation, it doesn't even have to be about business, just make a connection and try also to connect with them on either Facebook or LinkedIn.

   b. Find out where these people go to network or speak, and plan when you will attend these events.

   c. If you got a chance to speak to them about business, do you know what you would say? What is your 90 second pitch? What is your compelling offer?

2) How are you translating or conveying your brand message onto the social media channels?

   a. Think about what your message is and start to construct your own social media spider web.

    b. What do you want to be known for?

    c. List the social media channels that you believe will be most beneficial for your business.

    d. Go and create accounts at all of these on your list and connect them up on Ping.fm.

3) What are you currently doing, making or producing that is worth talking about?

    a. Once you have the spider web you need to populate it with conversation about what you are doing.

4) What is your personal style and what does it say about you?

    a. How can you improve it?

    b. Have you considered hiring an image consultant to help you with your personal brand?

5) List ten topics that you can easily talk about for 5-10 minutes in front of a video camera. For each topic, break down your short presentation into each of the following which will become your standard video presentation format:

    a. Part 1 – why would someone want to continue listening to what you are about to say. 30-60 seconds

    b. Part 2 – What is it you are about to explain and your reasons for explaining it. 2-3 minutes

    c. Part 3 – How to apply the information, this is the main content part of your topic. 3-5 minutes.

    d. Part 4 – Answer one or two questions that the listener might have by this point. 30-60 seconds.

    e. Part 5 – wrap up, conclude and include a call to action, e.g. Come visit our website for more information at www.mywebsite.com

6) Get a video camera and make these videos, which you've now planned out, then upload them onto a YouTube channel!

For more information on how you can improve your social media presence online, download a free report with the top seven ways right here: **www.llm.im/freestuff**

Notes

SECRET 10

Connect and become a Social Communicator

Being a social communicator is key to building your own profile online and giving people the perception of your 'fame'. The flip side to this, which I've already touched upon, is the power that this communication method has for your customers to continually spread good words about your services.

The one to one

As a customer, I like to know that I am dealing with a reputable company and part of that perception is created if I believe that company to be a large established company. This is especially relevant if you are selling a product.

It's easier for me to make a buying decision then because I know that even if I chose to return the product, or complain about the service, I would be able to safely assume that the company I chose would have procedures to handle these without me 'losing out' as such.

When I consider doing business on a website where I think the seller might be an independent, I know I am taking on a larger degree of risk as a buyer. Anything could happen, I might get the exact product I'm looking for, but then again I might just get nothing and see the website close down after a few weeks, losing all my money.

The interesting thing is, even though I want to deal with a large established company, I also at the same time want the personal attention and service I would get from an excellent independent company.

It's a tricky situation because if you are a large company you have to think about how you communicate at that personal level, conversely if you are a small, single-person company you want to be able to project a larger perception of your company to gain the trust and eventually the sale.

As a small company starting or growing up online, you are in a much better position because it is much easier to project a bigger brand and reputation online as a small company, than it is for an established company to change its ways and introduce personality and individuality to their online presence.

I said in an earlier chapter that the Internet is a one-to-one communication method and bearing this in mind is important to retain the personal nature of your online business.

Speaking to the individual

Your customer wants to feel that they are communicating with the people behind the website or social media front, so all your online language should reflect the personal nature. When customers feel that they are talking to someone 'real' per se, they are likely to build rapport even before you speak to them.

Avoid excessive use of group language in online communication and always imagine you are just chatting with your best friend. Make the language conversational and friendly as well as professional. It is possible to do both.

Treat the customer like they are the only customer that matters. Every customer is important and wants to feel like they are the special customer. Anything you can do to help that perception will add to your customer experience. These days customers aren't just looking to buy, they are looking for the complete customer experience.

Let me give you an idea of what that really means. The little things all add up to give the customer an overall incredible experience. I was out having dinner last night at a sushi restaurant and there were a couple of things that I thought would just make that tiny amount of difference and it would be negligible in terms of cost. Green tea is an extremely cheap drink to serve, so why not make it free and constantly keep the teapot topped up? It's the little things that matter. This place also served us complimentary fruit at the end of the meal.

I like to give my company as a great example of customer service. We make video one of our primary communication methods and integrate it heavily into our website. This is because most people won't read in full the content on a website; however they will sit and listen fully to a video. This makes it a better medium for introducing your services and conversions will increase significantly.

From the moment a customer takes on a project from my company, we will treat them with great respect and at every stage there are unique customer service things we do in order to keep them thinking 'wow'. At the end of the project we will give them a USB stick with the entire project in easy-to-understand folders. The USB stick has a welcome video from me on it to thank the customer and congratulate them on their project completion. We post them out a congratulations letter as well as vouchers that they can give to their friends.

We are at all times thinking about the customer experience and making it personal.

Activate word of mouth

Getting word-of-mouth marketing is the most effective marketing you could possibly do. Think about the times when you needed a plumber or electrician, it's likely that you first asked around your friends and family for recommendations. It's also likely that if you got a recommendation, you'd be using them instead of someone you found online or in the *Yellow Pages*.

What if you could get your customers to talk about you even when they aren't asked? Wouldn't that be the best marketing in the world? What about getting people to talk about your company who aren't even customers! That's what Zappos achieved, they not only activated their customers' word-of-mouth marketing, but they also activated non-customers to do word-of-mouth marketing. Now that is a trick that I think every company would like to learn.

This is clearly a challenging task indeed and the way Zappos did it was by being exceptional and being 'cool'.

I'd like to discuss a few ways in which you could use this strategy for yourself.

Making it cool to tell others

When something is cool, people want to tell their friends. This is because, for the most part, people are always seeking validation, and when you tell someone that something is cool, you are in fact saying, "I'm cool for telling you this." You're trying to demonstrate how cool you are.

Of course there is then the definition of cool, and what's cool within an industry can be very uncool in another. It's all about the context that you are talking from and to.

Of course you can use this if you find out what is perceived as 'cool' in your industry and then work some ideas around that. Be creative and think up some marketing campaign around that or how it could be integrated into your product or service and you'll start to have people talk about it.

Would you ever think that a mobile phone network could be 'cool'? Well, for a time T-Mobile achieved this through their flashmob advertising campaign. For those of you unfamiliar with what a flash mob is, it is used to describe a group of people who spontaneously get together in a public place to do wacky and sometimes ridiculously pointless acts for a short period of time and then disperse as if it never happened.

T-Mobile used this phenomenon to develop a marketing campaign where they choreographed an entire 3-minute dance routine with over 200 people spontaneously dancing in Liverpool Street station in London. The whole event was filmed and used as advertising. This video became incredibly viral and people were spreading the marketing without being prompted to. Their creativity in using this phenomenon to develop an advertising campaign has also been widely used elsewhere too.

On September 8th 2009 another well-executed flash mob was performed at Oprah Winfrey's 24th season kickoff party in Chicago where 21,000 of her fans performed an entire synchronised dance routine to the Black Eyed Peas single, *I Gotta Feeling*.

As you can imagine, there were hundreds of videos recorded of this event, from professional official sources to people in the street with their mobile phones. In total these videos have probably exceeded the hundreds of millions of views mark, going viral within minutes of it being shown live on TV, and literally spreading across the planet like wildfire. Imagine the marketing and exposure Oprah got for that! It's unimaginable.

Making it fun to tell others

Besides things being cool, the other common emotional hook is making something really fun or funny to activate that viral mechanism. Again the same psychological emotional hook is being employed here, that by passing on the fun stuff, people are in fact saying, "I'm a fun person for passing this on."

You probably don't want to admit it, however, I do the same thing and I think it's just what makes us human. The need to validate and gain acceptance from our peers, family and friends is important and essential to survival. Think about hundreds of thousands of years ago when humans lived in tribal society, the need to be accepted could mean in life or death. Now imagine that behaviour pattern being transferred across generations over tens of thousands of years and you can begin to understand how it forms the basis of our societies and civilisation, to the extent that our survival depends on it.

Anyways, diverging into evolution theory is not the objective here, just to illustrate how this plays into the equation of why people spread messages. Understanding its importance can help you to more intelligently create marketing around that and get why your message might or might not be spread.

So, making something fun and funny, using humour is an excellent way to get a message spread. Some of the funniest jokes, video clips and images have been spread so far around the planet that they have often become ingrained into common language too.

A fantastic example of using fun to spread the message is how Blendtec used YouTube to create a channel that to this date has had over 152million views. How did they do it? Well Blendtec is a company that makes food blenders and they are known to be the toughest, strongest blenders in the world, capable of blending anything. So what Blendtec did was to pose the question on their channel, "Will it Blend?", and made lots of videos showcasing items that were just silly and showed them being blended. They did the videos in a really fun, comedy way and there are videos of the machine blending items like iPhones, iPads, silly putty, laptops, car parts and lots more crazy things. If you're wondering whether those items really blended, go take a look yourself. The joky way this is done helped make it a viral channel and I'm sure has had an incredible response in terms of sales for their blender.

Another great use of viral video is the marketing campaign that Old Spice created with Isaiah Mustafa and gained an unbelievable 6.7 million views in the first 24 hours it was launched. That figure increased to over 23 million views in 36 hours. They created a parody of the ideal man in a bathroom set that changed design whilst Isaiah was still narrating the story. The videos are quite hard to describe, but one thing stands true, they are hilarious and have netted their channel nearly 200 million views.

The use of humour to spread the message is as old as you can imagine, so have a little fun and see where you can inject humour into your marketing ideas.

Making it profitable to tell others
When it comes to word-of-mouth marketing, it pays to give incentives to people who do pass on the word. Everybody likes a free gift, so when you tell your customers that they will receive a bonus gift for referring you to other people, be prepared for a flood of enquires.

These incentives could be anything from cash to credit, from food vouchers to free services. Just about any additional value you can give to your customers, they will certainly appreciate. You could create a cash back scheme or some sort of referral scheme that allows customers to accumulate referral credits which they can later redeem for more of your services.

There are many different ways in which you can implement a scheme that has the key objective of rewarding your clients for referrals.

Managing expectations

When it comes to what the customers expect, you can be assured that online their expectations are just as high as they would expect from any organisation, regardless of the fact that you might only be an online retailer.

As a company, you should be aiming towards always providing a consistent customer experience that is replicable and not over ambitious. Customers no longer perceive the online company to be any less professional than traditional companies; there have been so many successful implementations of high street brands online that customers now simply see the online shop as an extension of their buying experience.

What this means for new start-ups who are concentrating online, is that they need to start thinking like a company and stop delivering low level, amateur and unprofessional experiences through their websites.

There are many elements to keeping the customers' expectations met, including timely delivery of services or products, providing easy communication methods and ensuring standards are met.

In fact when you think about it, service standards today include much more than that of 5 years ago. The standards level is always moving and it's your job as an entrepreneur to define that level for your business and how it affects your overall performance.

Precision engineering

In the field of engineering there is a sub-discipline called precision engineering, which is primarily concerned with designing machines, fixtures and other structures that have exceptionally low tolerances, are repeatable and are stable over time.

These machines are required to have incredibly low tolerances for predictability, to be used in situations where safety and risk must be reduced to a minimum.

It isn't good enough just to have an incredible solution if the implementation of that solution you are providing is poor, uncontrolled and imprecise. By implementing your solution with the same methodology applied in precision engineering, you can ensure that the results will be the same every time which can add greatly to your customers' satisfaction each time they come back for repeat purchases.

The expectation customers have with regards to the details of your solution will be largely determined by how precise your implementation is. Swiss watches are notably known for their precision timing. You know that the watchmakers have spent a lot of time engineering their watches, the mechanics of the watch and every single component, to the highest accuracy possible. Every single metallic edge, every single cog, every single coil and metal surface has a reason for being where it is, how it is, the shape it is in order to combine together in a singular form which culminates in an accurate time piece.

Imagine your company is like a Swiss watch and ask those difficult questions to see if your system is as precise and well thought out as you know it should be. It's only when you've thought through all the fine details when your solution will be admired like many of the top Swiss watch brands.

When something is admired, it is talked about.

Experience tracking

The internet provides many fantastic tools and services that can help you to improve your solution, so using these to track customer experience is a great way to manage the whole process of serving the customer.

By implementing tracking at every stage of interaction with the customer, you can clearly identify sooner and quicker the places where communications break down and address them before they escalate to other customers.

Experience tracking is simply putting in markers at various stages of interaction that report whether the customer is engaged and potentially converting into a buyer. It's hard to actually measure engagement levels, so instead the way I recommend doing it is through communications tracking, the most vital point of which is when a customer stops wanting more information from you.

Having this in place will help you to tweak your service and experience to the levels of precision described above. As well as identifying problems sooner and being able to deal with them, it will also give you the ability to store buyer behaviour, in a similar way which supermarkets use reward cards to store your buying behaviours.

Workshop 10: Getting Others to Gossip

This is one of the hardest things to achieve in marketing, but the efforts you put in will be extremely worthwhile. I believe that by working on your marketing with a sole view to create a word-of-mouth campaign, you'll create a much more "sticky" talking point that will get your marketing and ultimately your brand, spread quicker with greater traction.

1) What makes your customer experience unique in comparison to your competitors?

2) What or how could you develop a marketing campaign that could make your solution look 'cool'?

3) What could be a way of adding fun into your marketing mix and creating something that people will want to spread?

4) Where in your business can you be more precise?

5) How can you create a reward system to compensate people who refer customers to you?

6) What can you do to track the online customer experience?

    a. Specifically how can you tell when a prospect is at the point of stopping communication with you?

Notes

_____

_____

_____

_____

_____

_____

_____

_____

_____

_____

_____

SECRET 11

Networking is not optional

Whenever people ask me what one single activity could I recommend that would change their entrepreneurial fortunes, the answer I always give is to go networking.

When I say networking, I mean more than just social networking online, I mean actually meeting people of your industry and meeting your potential customers wherever you think they might be.

I think for a lot of new entrepreneurs, the thought of networking is actually quite daunting, and I can sympathise because this was also one of my own personal fears. In the beginning, I didn't even think that it was necessary to network and for a while I believed that if you made something amazing, people would just find out about it naturally. I couldn't be more wrong.

It was in my 3rd year when I still wasn't making any money that I changed my way of thinking and started to go out networking. This simple act of going out to talk to people changed my entire fortunes for the better because there is so much value to be gained from other people doing the same thing as you, and from people who might be your customers.

My very first networking event was at a local greyhound racing venue and I was invited to a private event where I would be able to meet other affiliate marketers in my industry. At this event I met many people and the vast majority of people in this group were extremely high earners, people making the kind of money I was dreaming of.

Two things happened really, the first being that meeting people in this position helped me to realise how achievable my goals really were. When I met other people who had achieved what I wanted to achieve, it gave me the belief that I could actually succeed. The other thing I learnt was that people in the industry have an incredible amount of experience gained through their own efforts, and by sharing I learnt so many new ideas that I was inundated with new exciting ways to improve my website and its rankings.

I saw results immediately after implementing many of these ideas and from that point on I realised that networking was absolutely essential to success. It's still not my greatest strength to this day; however I do it because I know its value to me and my business. You must be prepared to do things you don't like doing in order to succeed.

What is online networking

By this point in the book I've already covered a lot of what online networking is, so I don't need to go into details about it all again.

Instead, let's summarize the top five benefits of online networking to refresh your memory about the areas you need to consider:

1. Online networking removes geographical boundaries and increases time efficiency. By networking online, you are able to reach the world from any computer or mobile device. Using the internet and email allows you to send messages to business counterparts during any time of the day from any location to be received anywhere around the world. The flexibility and practical aspects of connecting and building relationships expands target audiences, clients, customers, colleagues, vendors, partners, investors and even employees.

2. Online networking expands and diversifies your network. Online networking gives you a chance to develop relationships with several contacts at once. You can meet several people and communicate in a broader way than face to face or at a networking event by using technology like instant messaging or Skype. You can meet a wider variety of people through online networking. Usually, networking events will attract certain groups of people, depending on who is sponsoring the event. But with online networking, many different industries are represented within the group.

3. Online networking makes you more accessible to others. Having an online presence allows you the opportunity to be reached much more quickly than by phone and mail. Your ability to be accessible and reached easily allows your business to conduct its affairs more efficiently and productively. You are able to organise and execute projects and agendas in an efficient method, which can greatly affect your bottom line and give you a clear advantage over your competitors. It will also improve your credibility and image for your company, brand or service.

4. Online networking can be an excellent, low-cost marketing tool. One of the best advantages of online networking is the ability to profile you, company, product, services or brand. As an entrepreneur, I'm constantly looking for ways to create awareness and online networking offers that unique feature. Many websites allow members to post pictures, profiles, articles, books and various marketing materials for advertisements and announcements. You can use this to your advantage by posting and then linking back to them to show credibility to your clients.

5. Online networking allows you to develop and learn more skills. Many online networking groups or companies offers incentives and benefits to their members that can be extremely valuable to business and personal development. Blogs, articles, book recommendations, online seminars, teleseminars, announcements of local and national business events and

discounts on business publications or services, are just a few resources that entrepreneurs can use for success, which for the most part are generally first announced online.

How to be an effective offline networker

Other people have written entire books and series of books on how to get good at business networking, so if you are looking for an in-depth guide then I would certainly recommend you read those books. I've read many of those books in my career because I had to learn those skills from scratch.

What I want to touch upon is just the things that have worked for me and how it is beneficial to do more of them.

Direct Market Communication

One aspect of doing online business is that you are isolated, so quite often what I've personally experienced and also seen other online entrepreneurs do, is that they assume too much about the marketplace based on what they've read and researched.

I did exactly the same thing and for a while it didn't even occur to me that I needed to go out into the market place to learn about it from ground zero.

There are so many things that can be learnt from networking in the marketplace, lessons that cannot be learnt online. First off, you get to see the market in action and get to witness firsthand how suppliers interact with their customers. It doesn't matter what line of business you are setting up on the internet, there is always an offline place where people in the industry gather and there is always a place where your target customers are visiting.

People work best with trusted relationships and the best way to do that is to meet people. What appealed to me in the beginning about an online business was the fact that I thought I didn't have to go out and network. I was unskilled and afraid of how to behave in such situations. It wasn't until I started networking that I realised the power it had, and the effect it had on my business was substantial.

After my first forays into networking, I started to attend large conferences regularly and soon became a regular face at various events. Being at these events allowed me to see the suppliers in the market as well as possible customer types. It also gave me a chance to chat to affiliate programmes that were present and be able to discuss how the partnerships would work.

This had an incredible knock-on effect because something happens when people put a face to a name. They seem to develop an increased awareness of that company or person and the net result is that the whole relationship feels more 'real and the partnership develops and grows at an accelerated pace.

I've now put in a personal rule that if I haven't met in person the people who want to do business, I don't do business with them. Quite often we are called up in the office and there are people who want us to help them promote their products or services via affiliate programmes. Most of the time they are rejected as I haven't met them in person, however there are exceptions if the person is vetted by someone I trust highly.

Meeting the competition

When you start attending live events, whether those are conferences, seminars, specific networking events or any other method, you will get to meet the competition in your industry. You'll come face to face with the dreaded enemy and you'll have to start acting like a top secret spy to keep all your trade secrets. At least that's what I thought when I first started meeting my competition.

In fact, that perceived reality couldn't be further from the truth. Meeting the competition is an awesome thing to do because you will get to learn from each other. There are so many benefits from meeting your peers that to not do so, would in my opinion, prevent success overall.

Besides being able to learn from each other, you will also form peer-to-peer partnerships; there will be opportunities to trade information, skills and services. There is also the chance of increasing business through joint ventures.

The key here is that you should be listening more than you are talking. That doesn't mean you don't share your ideas and experience as well, it just means that you spend more time asking the right kind of questions and then also sharing your knowledge. You can't expect to have a good conversation without also being open to sharing your ideas.

Being friendly is also as important as being open. If you put on a great big smile and just have a friendly open attitude, you'll get to meet some of the top people in your industry and knowledge from these people can transform your entire business.

I remember in that very first networking event I went to, I had the fortune to meet a friendly guy whom I spent a large proportion of the evening chatting with. Keeping an honest and open conversation, he eventually introduced me to some other people he knew and these were some of the top people in the industry at the time. From that I managed to get into a private forum where the top strategies were discussed amongst the inner circle. I learnt new methods that I hadn't even considered and that single event caused a ripple effect throughout my business.

Of course being friendly also prevents other people from getting the wrong impression of you. You don't want to come across as that aggressive competitor; that doesn't serve you well.

The visual radar

When you get to a stage where you are looking for key partnerships to help accelerate your business, you'll need to develop a relationship with them that shows that you are someone they want to deal with.

There's no better way to start building this than by being in the visual radar of that person. The problem with the internet is that it is sense less; what I mean by this is that humans are sense-based creatures where our primary inputs are visual, auditory, kinaesthetic (touch), auditory digital (self-talk) and lastly gustatory (taste).

The only real sense you are hitting when you are communicating online is through the auditory digital channel, which represents the reader reading to themselves whatever you are communicating.

Your objective is to get them to remember you more easily such that they would consider it to be a relationship, yet you are only providing them with one means of remembering you. Think about the best memories you have about other people and just realise that you remember multiple things about them, what they say, what they look like, how they sound, how you feel when you are around them. These all make up part of your memory of them and then they become memorable.

So if there are people who you want to partner or do business with, you need to show up where they are. This means finding out what kind of events they attend and go there, it also means emailing them and then calling them for a 5-minute chat but most importantly it is about being visual and in front of them, even if all you say when you see them is a, "Hello".

Even if all you say to them is hello a few times, if you do this enough times then one day they will want to stop and talk to you to find out about you. Of course it's much quicker if you develop some conversation skills to initiate this communication sooner.

The trick here is to use a mechanism used in marketing, which is the 5-hour rule. In order for someone to have built up enough trust to deal with you, they must have spent 5 hours consuming your information, whether that is in one-to-one meetings, or whether they sat and watched your YouTube videos, or perhaps read a book you've written. Once that barrier is reached, you can safely request a sit-down meeting to discuss business and they will be open to the idea, at least enough to give you some of their time.

How offline connects with online

Clearly both types have to be done effectively so that you gain the maximum leverage with the activities. How they connect has already been mentioned a few times, however, in this next part I'll explain in a little more detail about the join.

Communication flow

One of the important aspects of networking is the flow of communication. Because businesses are more integrated than ever, you need to create an efficient system where the information you get offline flows easily and effortlessly into the online world for you to use.

The reverse must also be done so that your online communications flow effortlessly offline as well.

The reason for this is to maintain the congruency I spoke much about earlier. Part of the branding equation is in keeping a congruent message and maintaining consistency at all times. If you have a disjointed flow of your offline efforts and your online efforts, then this can break the continuity and present badly to potential customers.

You can be assured that the first thing a person does after meeting people is go back in their office, and when they are sitting down with a pile of business cards, they will do their due diligence online.

Your business card is an invitation to communicate and for most people now, the website is their first choice to investigate further. It doesn't require communication one to one and allows people to make an assessment of whether they would continue to do business with that person.

It's important to get this part right because over 85% of people will make their decision on whether to continue communication based on the quality of the website and whether they bother to look at your website is based on the quality of your business card.

So what really needs to flow? What I'm talking about is how information and communications flow between your emails to your printed literature, to things like your social media conversations. Is the same information being presented or do you have disjointed messages across the board?

What does your email signature say and what does your Twitter profile say about you? These are all part of the communication equation, so check the flow.

You are a real person

Networking shows people that you are a real person. I know it sounds kind of silly to state the obvious, however, the psychological aspects of it are very interesting and will greatly affect the success of your business.

These days, people are aware that many online profiles are fakes, even on Facebook. There are companies and individuals out there who are making lots of these online profiles to spam and market services, most relating to scam 'get rich quick' schemes.

People have become wary of them and just a simple visual meeting would help to alleviate this perception they might be having of you, if you are an online-only business.

Being real and present in networking also allows you to leverage your time more efficiently as you can be talking to several people at once, building that rapport on multiple levels with many different people all in the same time and environment. This is massively beneficial as this is almost impossible to do online. You can have conference calls, but that isn't really a rapport-building exercise, which is what you need at the beginning of a business relationship.

Technology driven

Linking your offline and online networking together also shows people that you are a forward thinking individual, embracing the technologies of tomorrow and moving with the times.

This simple perception can really help in today's business world when so many established small companies are being really slow in adopting these new communication methods, leaving them behind as customers are clearly seeking the best solution of today.

It's hard to believe that I've actually met people who have clearly said that they didn't need a website or any form of social media, even though they have also stated that they wanted to introduce an online element to their business.

To them, going online was getting an email address and allowing people to email them. When I would question further why they think they didn't need all the other elements, they would tell me that they wouldn't know how to manage it or run the technical side. They let their fears and limitations prevent them from seeing the bigger picture of how huge an impact it could be for their business.

5-hour meetings

This has been mentioned a few times already, about how you need the time element to build up that trust and credibility in a relationship to be able to begin talking more serious business.

I've read in some books about human communication that in general it takes approximately 4-6 hours before two people feel comfortable enough with their communication to take it to the next level. People need to feel a human connection before they will consider doing further business together.

In this aspect, with regards to online business, there are many ways you can use the internet to leverage that time and accelerate the whole process. Videos are a fantastic way for you to make up that time without being present. It provides the viewers with a sensory experience of you and that is almost as good as being there yourself.

Another way to spend more virtual time with your prospects is to produce things that take time for them to consume. For example you could write books, research, or articles and lead your potential customers to them. Think about it, a small book might take anything up to 3-4 hours to read, so that could be a large portion of the comfort building in just that one tool alone.

Other ways might include recording podcasts, audio interviews or audio educational content. Any form of sensory input will help to speed up the relationship-building process.

The end result of this is that generally people will feel like they know you, sometimes even before they have even met you.

I had experiences like this when I went to Fiji to attend a seminar in billionaire mindset training. Because it was such a huge trip for me to make and I had chosen to go around the world at the same time, I made a video diary of the trip, recording a video almost every day of the 28-day trip and uploading as soon as I could, each day.

By the time I reached Fiji, which was 13 days into the trip, there were other delegates at the training who had already seen my videos and commented on the journey I had been making. One said to me, "You're that guy from the UK going around the world aren't you?"

About 8 months later, I came back to this seminar, now held in Portugal and instead of participating I was helping out as a crew member. Whilst on registration day, a lady came up to me and said she couldn't believe that I was there.

It turns out that the reason she attended as a delegate was because she had watched all the videos I posted before about the seminar in Fiji and it was those videos that convinced her to come to Portugal.

I learnt something profound from those experiences, and that is that no matter how little value you think your content might be worth, someone else out there in the world will consider it to be highly valuable content. Your only obligation is to ensure you put it out there for the public to find.

Workshop 11: Identifying Networking Opportunities

1) What is the purpose for you when you go out networking?

    a. How does that serve your business needs?

    b. Think about what would happen if you didn't do it?

2) Where can you go to network? Write down a list of at least ten events you could attend in the next 2 months that are related to your industry.

3) What is the budget you have for networking? You need to think about this because networking does take some financial resources. You need to travel and sometimes events will have a ticket price, too. Assign yourself a monthly budget and stick to it.

4) How do you follow up with prospects once you've met them at a networking event?

    a. What do you do immediately to touch base?

    b. What do you do to keep track of the subsequent conversations?

5) What other materials could you provide that will help you to build up that trusted communication?

Notes

_____

_____

_____

_____

_____

_____

_____

_____

_____

_____

_____

_____

_____

_____

_____

SECRET 12

Leverage Outsourcers

This last chapter is really for those of you who have put everything in place, have seen some good results and you are now looking for ways to leverage your time to produce greater output and begin growing your business.

One of the themes throughout this book has been about obtaining the knowledge or finding the advice to help you build this internet business. I've always believed that if you don't know something, find someone who does know and learn everything you can from them, or have them do it for you. With the internet, you can now find anyone with any skill to do any job for you at any price.

As an entrepreneur I've spoken to many different business owners in varying stages of starting up new businesses and what consistently surprises me is how the majority of start-ups seem to have this low value on their time and then consistently complain about how little time they have to do everything they need to.

You know, you and I are no different to Oprah Winfrey or Lord Alan Sugar; we all have the same amount of time. This is the only resource on this plane of existence that we all have exactly the same of, so it's never a matter of having enough time, it's only a matter of what you do with the time you have.

It takes Teamwork to make your Dream work

Whenever I think of a team, a quote comes to mind from the famous basketball player Michael Jordan. He said, "Talent wins games, but teamwork and intelligence wins championships."

It's true to say that without a strong team you are never going to become hugely successful because you simply can't do everything you need to do by yourself.

I think a fundamental flaw in new entrepreneurs is that they often believe that they can do everything themselves. I know for myself I certainly thought like this for a long while, and I would always think that no matter how good someone else was, I could do a task better and more effectively.

Besides the low value placed on time, start-up entrepreneurs also seem to think they are Supermen and can do everything by themselves, oftentimes to prove something to someone.

What I've witnessed and learnt from my own experience and from studying other successful entrepreneurs is that the really super-successful entrepreneurs have the complete opposite mindset in that they get outside assistance and additional manpower help the moment they can justify it. In most cases it's almost straight away, even before they have made a profit.

This uncanny disregard for common fears is what excels these exceptional entrepreneurs to levels of success that we mere mortals could only dream of. The Google Twins each became multi-billionaires within a decade. It took Lord Alan Sugar most of his life so far, approximately 40 years, to amass just $1bn in comparison.

Despite the massive difference, both parties had from the beginning employed teams of people to help them to succeed and this is something that you must also challenge yourself to do early on. I think there is a false perception that having an online business means it's all easy and you can do it all yourself, where that comes from I'm not sure, but one thing I am sure of, any business that is successful, no matter online or offline, has a team.

I made that mistake very early on, in fact I was so comfortable doing everything by myself that I had forgotten how to be an entrepreneur and I became a robotic mechanic, doing the same thing over and over again to maintain the results I had achieved. I hit a ceiling to the amount I could earn and it was only then in my 7th year of running that I started to build resources around me, having overcome my own limiting beliefs and fears around having staff.

You are nothing without your team.

Shoot for the stars

There's a saying that goes something like this, shoot for the stars and land on the moon, shoot for the moon and land back on earth. What it means for me is that you have to aim high and even if you don't hit your target, you'll land somewhere great; if you set your targets too low, you'll just end up where you started.

This couldn't be more apt when it comes to finding team members. I prefer to call my staff 'team members' because it is a team effort and the word employee is just so uninspiring. You must aim to find star people to help you in your organisation because quite simply, star players will attract to them star players and produce incredible work together.

It's interesting to observe that average players will attract other average players and together produce less than average results. Hold yourself to high standards and do not hold back on hiring the best people you can.

Another reason for hiring key star people into your team is that once you have someone inside your organisation, it's much harder to get rid of them than you can imagine. Here in the UK, there are so many laws protecting employees that you have to be careful who you employ otherwise you could just be stuck with them for a while, just like the white elephants you have in your house.

I learnt this mistake too; I seem to learn all the mistakes by actually experiencing them! That's why I'm writing this book so that you can avoid all those disastrous decisions I made that cost me years in business growth.

The mistake I made was that I hired someone without doing my proper due diligence and interview process. No matter how small your company is, you have to do proper interviews and get to the guts of the person you intend to hire. It is so vital that you get a complete picture of the person before you commit to bringing them on board.

If the role is a technical role, devise a test. If the role is a support role, have them trial for a few days as part of the interview process. Whatever the positions are, you must always test and delve further into them as a person.

This means also to find out about their personal history and also their life dreams, goals and vision of the world. You might not think this is vital, however if you are building a long-term business and you hope to sustain a singular congruent message across the company, you must ensure that the people you hire are also aligned to your mission.

What is your hourly rate?

Delving further into the question of what your hourly rate is, think about what your time is worth to you right now. Is your time worth £10 an hour or perhaps it's worth £500 an hour? Only you can make a judgement on what value you're worth and this will partly be based on the income you are generating, and the potential income you could be making.

The reason why this is so important is that right from the beginning entrepreneurs have a funny habit of ripping themselves off.

That's right, from the very beginning most entrepreneurs will rip themselves off day after day because they haven't valued their time enough.

I'll give you a basic example to illustrate. Say you valued your time at £50 per hour; perhaps this is the rate you could consult at. What would you value a house cleaner's hour rate at? I'd say you can get a decent cleaner for £10 an hour and probably less. So if you are still doing your own house cleaning, you are literally ripping yourself off by £40 every hour you spend cleaning your living/working space.

Do you still do your own grocery shopping? How long does it take? After you've made the journey there and parked, then meandered around the food aisles remembering what to buy, somehow you always end up walking down every single aisle to make sure you haven't missed anything. Then as you're leaving you might decide to fill up the petrol as well. In total you've probably spent at least 2 hours shopping.

If you did it online you can do it in about 30 minutes, you log on and find that the online store has all your favourites listed for easy access, all you do is add them to your cart, enter your card details and book your delivery slot. It doesn't take more than 30 minutes, if you buy regularly it'll reduce to 15 minutes and even less than that.

Let's presume you did a shop every 2 weeks, that's 26 times a year you'd be shopping for food, which means in person you'd have spent about 52 hours shopping. If you value your time at £50 per hour, that's £2600 worth of time value spent going shopping for food.

If you bought online only, delivery at £5 each delivery will cost you £130 and you'd save yourself 39 hours of shipping time. That's a saving of £1950, less the cost of delivery will give you a total saving of £1820. I bet you didn't think about shopping in that way.

You can easily apply this to all the tasks in your life and soon you'll realise how often you rip yourself off. We've all done it before, we entrepreneurs think that we are Supermen, remember. When I'm asked what position I hold in my company I often joke that I'm the CEO, Chief of Everything Officer, I'm the founder, the programmer, the salesman, the janitor and the company mascot.

Do the right thing, start to see where you can get help and stop ripping yourself off.

The internet economy

The fact that you can communicate with anyone in the world, no matter what language you all speak, gives everyone a level playing field and this has meant a dramatic reduction in service costs worldwide.

What this means is that you can find services much cheaper that you could find locally. Whatever those services are, whether that is man power to do data entry, or some design service, it can all be found cheaper online somewhere out there in the world.

The most effective use of this dynamic for internet-based businesses is levering technical talent. I believe this is the best use because technical work online has a strict set of rules. Programming has explicit code and it doesn't matter if you are English, American, Chinese or African, you would all programme exactly the same code. So the only difficulty is in communicating the requirements such that they are understood and overcoming cultural barriers. The work itself can be achieved regardless of culture, location or language.

This is an extremely interesting development in global access because it means that you can effectively employ people from anywhere in the world; you won't even be bound by UK employment laws as hiring virtual workers abroad typically means you are just operating under a standard service level agreement.

How far does a penny go?

Global economics plays a massive role in internet businesses because the cost savings you can make are so great that it makes even micro-niche ideas viable in a country where otherwise it might have been too costly to deliver.

Being based in the UK is a pretty powerful position to be in terms of international internet business because our pound sterling goes a long way in most other countries of the world. We have the potential here to lead internet business because of our strong currency position.

If I wanted to hire a full-time web developer here in the UK, it would cost me around £28,000 for someone who has perhaps a few years' experience and isn't straight out of university. Big organisations will even pay up to £40,000 for the best graduates, as they know the value of excellence.

I think it will shock you to know that for £28,000, I can hire 50 same-level web developers in India or the Philippines, working for me full time, and I would be paying them double what they would get paid by a local employer. It's not a typo, you read it right, that's 50 people I can hire for the same cost. Of course with those numbers I would now have to hire managers and team leaders etc, but that's beside the point.

Your money goes an incredibly long way in other countries and now you can benefit from this opportunity.

What's even more outstanding as a development is that because of the recognised cost savings abroad, local service suppliers have now also dropped their prices in order to stay in business and compete; some people are still willing to pay a little bit more for local suppliers, but they will not be prepared to pay ridiculous amounts anymore.

This means that there are a growing number of affordable local suppliers, too, on the market and quite often you'll find them on outsourcing websites like Odesk, Elance or PeoplePerHour. There are many reasons why local suppliers are popping up and part of that is many people are providing services as a means of earning extra income.

They could be women on maternity leave at home, people with mobility disabilities, retired workers, housewives, unemployed or redundant workers. There are so many opportunities out there that all it takes is a little ingenuity and you've got yourself a small online business.

Welcome to the world of virtual workers

This is perhaps one of the most exciting times on the planet when we can literally build entire businesses from our own homes and run a company with multiple team members, without even needing to see your team.

It's all possible now with the plethora of services and communication methods available online. We are without a doubt entering into a new age of communication, working and global cooperation, where we as entrepreneurs can really help to draw talent from anywhere and equally spread the wealth back to places where otherwise it was impossible to do so 15 years ago.

By employing for example someone in Romania or Indonesia, you are dramatically improving their lives with your contribution and this will drive further advances in each of those regions as more of the same activities occur worldwide. Global wealth is truly being distributed in a fair and equal manner.

These kind of substantial shifts in service delivery means that we are for the first time entering into a virtuous circle of providing true value to everyone involved in delivering the solution. Not only is the customer getting real value for money services, the team members are all getting well compensated and working in environments that are more organic and less rule bound like they are in typical office structures.

The result is that everyone is happier and living a more fulfilled life, being able to be judged on their results, not on how well they can run the treadmill of corporate dictation. It means people are free to pursue their own lives in conjunction with their work and perhaps the two are actually aligned since both parties willingly came together through choice.

No longer will incentives be required to drive team members forward, the carrot and stick is an old industrial age mechanism that no longer works in the information age. People are driven by cause and mission and being a part of something that is greater than themselves.

The most dangerous beasts of the land

The fantastic thing about having a virtual team is that the old problem of office politics being a negative force within companies becomes more or less muted as the dynamics for it happening no longer exist.

Out in the wild there are these other beasts battling it out for ultimate supremacy, the big Bureaucracy Lion versus the Office Politics Mosquito.

How does a lion behave? Well, lions spend much of their time resting and are inactive for about 20 hours per day. Although lions can be active at any time, their activity generally peaks after dusk with a period of socialising, grooming, and defecating. Intermittent bursts of activity follow through the night hours until dawn, when hunting most often takes place. They spend an average of two hours a day walking and 50 minutes eating. That sounds a lot like the way bureaucrats behave!

What about mosquitoes? They are the world's number one killer animal only because of the fact that they spread malaria to both animals and humans. There are hoards of mosquitoes across the planet and although their bite is often harmless, it can still sting and in the worst cases it will transmit deadly diseases. Sounds a bit like office politics to me.

Virtual working will more or less bring office politics to an end; if the same attitude of global communication and coordinated planned effort was made to eliminate malaria, I'm positive that it would be equally as effective.

The big giant bureaucracy lion can also be tamed by giving people the autonomy that is experienced by virtual working.

In my own tale of espionage and under-the-table deals, my personal reasons for leaving to become an entrepreneur were also to do with all the office politics and bureaucracy in the organisations I worked for. In the end I decided that I could determine my own fate and not leave it up to the mechanistic rule of corporate dictators.

It's good for you, your team and our planet

Perhaps you haven't considered that running a virtual team is in fact doing the planet some good as well. By reducing the need for fixed costs such as lighting, office space, land area, and other overhead costs, you are also reducing your overall carbon footprint on the planet.

An office is where people gather together to work, yet for most of the time on this planet, office spaces are bare and barren, all the time taking up resources and energy. By each person making maximum use of his environment and space you are reducing that burden on society.

In a study done by the US Bureau of Labor Statistics, they calculated that office space in the USA was empty almost 50% of the time, and that statistic was not including out-of-office hours!

It goes much further than this, in that what is good for you is also good for your team and even better for the planet.

Let's take a case study to examine the cost benefits of running a five-man virtual team versus running a small office of 5 people and see how much is saved. Just to be clear up front, this is a general example, so details and specific costs may vary across cities and countries, plus the cost of wages is not included in this calculation because we are comparing fixed costs, not talent costs.

To run a small office for five people you would probably need a space of about 1000 sq feet with amenities to service them, including a small kitchen, break area, toilets, storage and server rooms. You'd then need to kit out the whole place with furniture and supply workstations for each team member as well as pay for running costs such as electricity, water and heating.

Rather than get all statistical with numbers, you can research all of this online, but I can tell you that the cost of the space alone would be on average around £50,000 for the year. I've estimated a further £25,000 for setting up the space with the required amenities and services as well as computer equipment. That's a quite conservative estimate of £75,000 fixed cost.

Let's compare that with running a virtual team of five where everyone is working from their own homes or own workspaces. There's no need for an office and service costs are absorbed by the worker in their own costs. This can of course be reimbursed through salary if that is the chosen business model.

You would probably need to supply them with computing equipment and have a small space yourself to maintain the main server. You could however choose to outsource this component completely as well. The cost of this would be about £1500 for a high-end laptop or workstation, and about £250 per person running costs for mobile phone and internet costs for the worker. That's a total cost of about £22,500.

Clearly these are just sample figures, however, you can see that there will still be a considerable saving of £52,500 and more importantly a reduced environmental impact. What could you do with an extra £52,500 in your business if you could save that by running the company with efficiency in mind?

Your problems just got better

Your problems don't go away they just get better over time. What to do with the extra time is a better problem to have than not having enough time to do what you want!

This is what we've been aiming for the whole time, making more time to do the things we want to do. It was never about the money was it? It was always about what the money could do for you in terms of time and opportunity.

You know as well as I do that this is the moment, the moment when you've reached this point where you are in a position to choose what to do with the time you now have for yourself.

The efforts you've put in have culminated in success and your ability to leverage outsourcers and virtual teams has earned you the dream life that you have been visualising all the time.

Now is the time when you will take your new internet business to new levels, building upon its success and driving forward to create even more growth and deliver even more value to your customers than ever before.

With this time you've now created for yourself, you can take a moment to relax and celebrate your success. Then take a deep breath and get yourself ready for the next part, how to grow your business into the seven-figure mark.

Workshop 12: Time to Make Time

It's time to consider how you can begin to grow your online business now that you've had some success.

1) Consider what key roles within your company would need to be filled in order help your company grow?

    a. Who would be your first key hires?

    b. What roles would you want to fill because you are weakest in this area?

2) Calculate the cost of your current lifestyle in terms of what you spend your time doing, and then ask yourself if there are people or services you could hire who could take that burden away from you.

    a. What is your hourly rate?

    b. What area of your life do you need help in?

3) A thought question, how virtual can your operation get?

4) Calculate the fixed cost to you if you hired a virtual employee.

For a complete audio guide on all the workshops in this book, go to **www.llm.im/freestuff**

Notes

What is with the Elephants and Speedlights stories?

There are lessons to be learned ALL THE TIME in business and I can vouch for the fact that life is a never ending learning curve. In the first version of this book, I titled it Speedlights and Elephants: Winning the Online Business Game because I wanted to create a title that was different and memorable. I achieved that, but I also failed to recognise that when it comes to searching for the book, it made it nigh on impossible.

What I learnt is that sometimes you have to be blatantly obvious about your intentions, or in this case what the book's intentions were. This is a business strategy and mindset book, and not some quirky novel.

I did however leave the fun images in the book as I do think even though business is a serious thing, we should all remember to have fun with it.

Hindsight is a great thing, and often in life we don't get a second chance at certain things, so since I had the chance to amend this book to a second version, I made a better more informed choice as to the design and book title.

Why Speedlights?

I used the term speedlights to symbolize all the fun and inspiring part of being an entrepreneur. For me, it is my favourite piece of equipment in photography because it gives me the ability to control light, and photography is all about capturing light in all its many forms.

When you are starting out in business, be that online or offline, you have to be in control of your company at all times. The vision that you have for your business can only be realised by yourself, no matter who is helping you, or who has invested in you. If you watch *Dragons Den*, no matter how much the Dragons choose to invest, the qualities they are always looking for are character, personality and vision.

If you told Edison that one day he'd be able to flash an incredibly strong beam of controlled light many times a minute, he'd probably tell you it's possible, but not in his era! Well he'd be right because that's what the speedlight is, a portable sun machine. The sun is one of the most powerful forces in our solar system, and it is a contributor in the whole grand design of our planet. To think that we have devices which can yield this power is incredible.

You are the same; those flashes of creativity and inspiration in your minds are equally as powerful as the rays of the sun, or indeed my speedlight. With these flashes, you can create greatness in your life and leave this planet a better place as well.

What about the elephants?

Elephants are strong creatures; they have long lives and never forget anything. You want your business to have many flashlight moments because these are the inspirational times when ideas are flying, but at the same time you also want to build your business like an elephant, strong and stable.

Elephants are notoriously difficult to tame and train as well. With training systems that have been developed over thousands of years, they are carefully broken in and then taught to respond to its master's instructions. The master, also known as a mahout, combines both strict training regimes and total love and care in order to get the elephant used to them, trusting them and obeying their commands.

In much the same way, your business is your elephant, you want to apply love and care to it yet at the same time you need to be disciplined and regimented. Once you have tamed your business, you have it under your full control and you'll then have a strong and powerful force behind you, building up slowly, with strength and longevity.

An elephant never forgets, so the saying goes. This has actually been backed up by studies in science and to a large degree it's true. Just like an elephant, too, you want your business to never forget. What I mean by this, is that if you have set up the company properly, collecting statistics on your web traffic, maintaining correct official legal records and accounting records, then effectively your business hasn't forgotten anything, a strong position to be in when the tax man decides to pay a visit.

In the end, you want your business to be the biggest company in your industry sector, in the same way the elephant is the largest land mammal on our planet.

Conclusion: Feel amazed, empowered and ready

I was amazed at myself for having achieved so much in such little time. From the moment I read the article through to seeing my first commercial website on the screen, I realise that I had taught myself web design, web programming and lots of other skills as well to get the whole thing working online.

Sometimes we can do amazing things when we put our minds to it and I guess being in debt at the time also motivated me to get into gear, get over my fears and take action towards my goals that I had set.

What was even more amazing was how I felt; even though I hadn't yet made any money through this new website, I had a feeling of certainty and pride that I was finally taking control in my own life. It felt wonderful and I felt totally empowered because I had taught myself more than the technical skills, I had taught myself to overcome my own fears and to take action.

It was the same feeling I had when I was sitting in Cairo Airport, ready to depart the country after I had the best trip of my life. After that scary incident at immigration, everything was ok in the end and they let me pass but not without me spending 45 minutes sweating. I guess there's a lesson to be learnt from all that, be prepared whatever you do.

The trip itself was amazing and totally empowering as each day I spent backpacking with the group I joined, I discovered more and more what I was capable of when I push myself to the absolute limits of my own comfort. Throughout the trip, I had helped our main leader keep people organised and I brought a positive energy to the group which people loved: it showed me that I was a natural leader.

On this trip I had visited the Pyramids, the Valley of the kings, taken a midnight hike up to the top of Mt Sinai to watch sunrise, snorkelled for the first time in my life (I'm an incredibly weak swimmer, but I had to go for it), slept overnight on a beach and made some amazing friends along the way.

Reflecting on the trip and what I had learnt, I sat in the airport lounge and soon I heard a call for our flight leaving, so I got up and walked towards the departure terminal...

...As I stepped through I had a feeling run through me, I was ready for this.

Even though I had only 1 year of professional photography experience, I was confident in my own ability and overall I had a knowing feeling of being ready to tackle the day.

The hairdressers were already working with the three models and I went and said hello to everyone whilst they were going about their preparations. The day didn't run as smoothly as I would have liked, but that didn't matter because whatever challenges came about, there was always a solution; I just had to think quickly and take strong positive action. The radio trigger failed and I had to quickly go to a local shop to find a replacement solution. This was the controlling mechanism for my trusty speedlight, which I was relying on to get my creative shots. Thankfully there was a way around the problem using a corded trigger. Also, the studio lights we brought to the set weren't bright enough so we had to make do with what we had available and get really creative in the use of natural light.

When the day was finally over I remember sitting down back at home and thinking to myself, what a wonderful day. I didn't think I was ready to attempt such an audacious photo shoot so early in my photography career, but it didn't matter. What I learnt was that you are as ready as you want to be.

Whether you think you are ready to build an internet business or not, I can tell you that you are ready right now and the sooner you start, the sooner you'll create the life of your dreams.

Bibliography/Notes

- Wikionomics: How mass collaboration changes everything – Don Taspcott & Anthony D. Williams

- The 22 Immutable Laws of Branding – Al Ries and Laura Ries

- Key Person of Influence – Daniel Priestley

- Think and Grow Rich – Napoleon Hill

- Business Stripped Bare – Richard Branson

- Altitude – Eben Pagan

- Outliers & The Tipping Point – Malcolm Gladwell

- www.techradar.com

- www.techcrunch.com

- Freakonomics – Steven d. Levitt & Stephen J. Dubner

- Purple Cow & Tribes – Seth Godin

- Generations – William Strauss

- The Selfish Gene – Richard Dawkins

What is Mindlogr?

In my latest venture I've been developing a software platform called Mindlogr which allows people to go online and create private video journals.

Since I'm a big advocate of journaling as a means to learning more about self and mind, I decided to make something to help people do this more easily.

The platform essentially is a private version of Youtube with tools and features that have been designed specifically for private recording.

People are using the platform to create journals and diaries on various topics including:

- private life video journals
- diet journals
- fitness videos
- practice musical instruments
- record their family history

Amongst all, what it's give people is a place where they can truly be themselves and let go of any tension and stress in their lives.

Take a look and see what you think.

www.mindlogr.com

Author Biog

After working for various companies from blue chips like British Aerospace, CSC and a range of smaller financial software companies, Eddie began his entrepreneurial career in 2001 venturing into the digital marketing space.

Early successes in digital marketing, specifically SEO and affiliate marketing lead him towards forming a full time digital agency in 2004 which he has been running since. Named, Lady Luck Media, he produced several revenue generating websites in the affiliate marketing world and is considered to be one of the top SEO experts in the field.

Since then, Lady Luck Media became a highly skilled niche company focussing on search engine optimisation, high impact conversion strategies and low expenditure high yield traffic campaigns. From 2004 to present day, Eddie has personally generated over £6m revenue using these new online marketing tools and strategies.

In 2008, the company took another focus to engage and help other Entrepreneurs to create the kind of success that Eddie had created from a starting budget of zero. His personal learning and growth also took him into the coaching fields where he trained in Neuro-Linguistic Programming, and is now a Master NLP Practitioner.

From 2012, Eddie felt another calling towards technology and started to devote his time to creating new ventures in the field of online video technology. He is currently the founder of Mindlogr, a private video logging platform that provides users with a place where they can record time capsule memories of their lives and thoughts.

Notes

Notes

Notes

Notes

Made in the USA
Middletown, DE
25 February 2016